For Reference

Do Not Take From the Library

W9-CLM-304

OUTLAWS, MOBSTERS & CROOKS

OUTLAWS, MOBSTERS & CROOKS

From the Old West to the Internet

VOLUME 3

Bandits & Gunslingers

•

Bootleggers

•

Pirates

Marie J. MacNee

Edited by Jane Hoehner

U·X·L ®

AN IMPRINT OF GALE

DETROIT · NEW YORK · LONDON

This book is dedicated, with love, to my parents

OUTLAWS, MOBSTERS & CROOKS: FROM THE OLD WEST TO THE INTERNET

by Marie J. MacNee

STAFF

Jane Hoehner, *U·X·L Senior Editor*
Carol DeKane Nagel, *U·X·L Managing Editor*
Thomas L. Romig, *U·X·L Publisher*

Shanna Heilveil, *Production Associate*
Evi Seoud, *Assistant Production Manager*
Mary Beth Trimper, *Production Director*

Jessica L. Ulrich, *Permissions Associate*
Margaret Chamberlain, *Permissions Specialist*

Michelle DiMercurio, *Art Director*
Tracey Rowens, *Senior Art Director*
Cynthia Baldwin, *Product Design Manager*
Barbara J. Yarrow, *Graphic Services Supervisor*

Marco Di Vita, Graphix Group, *Typesetting*

LIBRARY OF CONGRESS CATALOGING-IN-PUBLICATION DATA

MacNee, Marie J.
    Outlaws, mobsters & crooks: from the Old West to the Internet /
Marie J. MacNee : edited by Jane Hoehner.
        p. cm.
    Includes bibliographical references (p.   ) and index.
    Contents: v. 1. Mobsters, racketeers and gamblers, robbers — v.
2. Computer criminals, spies, swindlers, terrorists — v. 3. Bandits
and gunslingers, bootleggers, pirates.
    Summary: Presents the lives of seventy-five North American
criminals including the nature of their crimes, their motivations,
and information relating to the law officers who challenged them.
        ISBN 0-7876-2803-4 (set : acid-free paper). — ISBN 0-7876-2804-2
(vol. 1 : acid-free paper). — ISBN 0-7876-2805-0 (vol. 2 : acid
free paper). —ISBN 0-7876-2806-9 (vol. 3 : acid-free paper)
        1. Criminals—North America—Biography—Juvenile literature.
[1. Criminals.]   I. Hoehner, Jane.   II. Title.   III. Title:
Outlaws, mobsters, and crooks.
    HV6245.M232   1998
    354.1'097—DC21   98-14861
                                                                    CIP
                                                                    AC

Contents

Volume 1

VOLUME 2

VOLUME 3

Reader's Guide

"History is nothing more than a tableau of crimes and misfortunes," wrote eighteenth-century French writer Voltaire. There certainly is more to history than criminal deeds, misdemeanors, and misfortunes, but these offenses do offer fascinating lessons in history. The life stories of outlaws provide a glimpse into other times and other places, as well as provocative insight into contemporary issues.

Who's Included

Outlaws, Mobsters & Crooks: From the Old West to the Internet presents the life stories of seventy-three outlaws who lived (or committed crimes) in North America from the seventeenth century to the present day—from Blackbeard, the British-born pirate who terrorized the Carolina coast, to terrorist Timothy McVeigh.

Everyone's familiar with Bonnie and Clyde, Butch Cassidy, and Al Capone. But how many know the *whole* story: what their childhoods were like, what their first crime was, who worked with them—and against them—and how they ended up? *Outlaws, Mobsters & Crooks* offers a thorough and provocative look at the people and events involved in these stories.

Familiar figures such as Jesse James and Billy the Kid are present, as are lesser-known outlaws whose careers reveal much about the times in which they lived. Cattle Kate, for instance, was little more than a cattle rustler, but her story provides insight into the cattle wars of nineteenth-century Nebraska and the tensions that led to the Lincoln County War. Also included are outlaws such as Calamity Jane, whose main crime was unconventionality, and lawmen who sometimes stood on the wrong side of the law. The many men and women who have been labeled outlaws over the course of three centuries cannot all be profiled in one three-volume work. But those whose stories are told in *Outlaws, Mobsters & Crooks* include some of the best known, least known, weirdest, scariest, most despised, and least understood outlaws. In short, this work is intended as an overview of North American criminals—a jumping-off point for further inquiry.

LEGENDS, MYTHS, AND OUTRIGHT LIES

Many of the men and women profiled have been surrounded by legends that have grown to enormous proportions, making it very difficult to separate fact from fiction: Billy the Kid killed one man for every year of his life (he probably killed no more than six men); Jesse James lived to old age as a gentleman farmer (he was shot in the back of the head by Robert Ford at the age of thirty-four); Black Hand extortionists could bring bad luck to their victims simply by giving them "the evil eye" (they brought them bad luck, all right, but it was usually accomplished with a gun). In some cases, legends have fed on the published accounts of the criminals themselves—or the lawmen who pursued them. Some are accurate first-person accounts. Others are sensational exaggerations of true events—or wholesale fabrications. *Outlaws, Mobsters & Crooks* attempts to present a fair and complete picture of what is known about the lives and activities of the seventy-three outlaws profiled. When appropriate, entries mention the myths, unconventional theories, and alternate versions of accepted history that surround a particular outlaw—without suggesting they are truthful or fact-based.

ARRANGEMENT AND PRESENTATION

Outlaws, Mobsters & Crooks is arranged into three volumes. To enhance the usefulness of these volumes, the seventy-three entries have been grouped into ten categories: Mobsters, Racketeers and Gamblers, and Robbers (Volume 1); Computer Criminals, Spies, Swindlers, and Terrorists (Volume 2); and Bandits and Gunslingers, Bootleggers, and Pirates (Volume 3). Within each category, entries—which range from three to eleven pages in length—are arranged alphabetically by the outlaw's last name. The only exceptions to this arrangement are those outlaws who are listed by their "common" name, such as Billy the Kid or Black Bart; these entries are listed alphabetically by the first letter in that name. Aliases and birth names are presented when available. Each entry includes the birth and death dates of the subject (or the period during which he, she, or the gang was active).

Entries are lively, easy to read, and written in a straightforward style that is geared to challenge—but not frustrate—students. Difficult words are defined within the text; some words also include pronunciations. Technical words and legal terms are also explained within entries, enabling students to learn the vocabulary appropriate to a particular subject without having to consult other sources for definitions.

WHAT'S INSIDE

A detailed look at what they did, why they did it, and how their stories ended. Entries focus on the entire picture—not just the headline news—to provide the following sorts of information:

- **Personal background:** interesting details about the subject's family, upbringing, and youth

- **Crimes and misdeeds:** an in-depth look at the subject's outlaw history

- **Aftermath:** from jail time, to legal and illegal executions, to mysterious disappearances, entries relate what happened after the dirty deeds were done

- **A look at the other side of the law:** Many entries also provide extensive information on the other side of the law, for example, the brilliant astronomer who tracked a West German hacker, the FBI agents who hounded John Dillinger and Al Capone, and the frontier judge who earned the nickname "the hanging judge."

ADDED FEATURES

Outlaws, Mobsters & Crooks includes a number of additional features that help make the connection between people, places, and historic events.

- A timeline at the beginning of each volume provides a listing of outlaw landmarks and important international events.

- Sidebars provide fascinating supplemental information, such as sketches of criminal associates, profiles of law enforcement officials and agencies, and explanations of the political and social scenes of the era, for example, the anti-communist hysteria that consumed the United States at the time of the Rosenberg trial. Sidebars also offer a contemporary perspective of people and events through excerpts of letters written by the outlaw profiled, citations from newspapers and journals of the day, and much more.

- Quotes—both by and about the outlaw—offer revealing insights into their lives and times.

- 117 photographs and illustrations bring the outlaws to life.

- Suggestions for related books and movies—both fictional and fact-based—are liberally sprinkled throughout the entries.

- A list of sources for further reading at the end of each entry lists books, newspaper and magazine articles, and Internet addresses for additional and bibliographical information.

- A comprehensive index at the end of each volume provides easy access to the people, places, and events mentioned throughout *Outlaws, Mobsters & Crooks: From the Old West to the Internet.*

SPECIAL THANKS

The author would like to thank U•X•L Senior Editor Jane Hoehner, Permissions Associate Jessica L. Ulrich, and the research staff—particularly Maureen Richards—of Gale Research for their invaluable help and guidance. The author would also like to thank the staff of the Grosse Pointe Library for their gracious assistance.

COMMENTS AND SUGGESTIONS

We welcome your comments on this work as well as suggestions for personalities to be featured in future editions of *Outlaws, Mobsters & Crooks: From the Old West to the Internet.* Please write: Editors, *Outlaws, Mobsters & Crooks,* U•X•L, 835 Penobscot Building, Detroit, Michigan, 48226-4094; call toll-free: 1 (800) 877-4253; or fax (313) 877-6348.

Outlaws Alphabetically

Italic number indicates volume number

Timeline

Spring 1718: Edward Teach—also known as **Blackbeard**—and his crew of pirates blockade the city of Charleston, South Carolina.

November 1718: Thomas Spotswood, the governor of Virginia, issues a proclamation offering rewards for the capture—dead or alive—of **Blackbeard** and his shipmates.

November 22, 1718: A navy crew led by Lieutenant Robert Maynard attacks **Blackbeard**'s pirate ship near the Carolina coast. The severed head of Blackbeard is hung from the bowsprit of the navy ship.

1720: Captain Woodes Rogers, the governor of the Bahamas, issues a proclamation naming Calico Jack Rackam, **Anne Bonny,** and Mary Read as enemies of England.

May 9, 1800: Joseph Baker and two other pirates are hanged in a public execution in Philadelphia, Pennsylvania.

March 11, 1831: Charles Gibbs and Thomas G. Wansley are convicted of murder and piracy in New York.

March 19, 1831: An Englishman named Edward Smith commits the first bank heist in American history when he robs the City Bank in New York City.

April 22, 1831: Pirates **Charles Gibbs** and Thomas G. Wansley are hanged on Ellis Island in New York in front of thousands of onlookers.

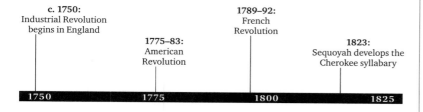

c. 1750:
Industrial Revolution
begins in England

1775–83:
American
Revolution

1789–92:
French
Revolution

1823:
Sequoyah develops the
Cherokee syllabary

1750   1775   1800   1825

July 11, 1859: Gold thief **Richard Barter** is shot and killed by Sheriff J. Boggs in the California foothills.

1861: Shortly after the Civil War breaks out, **Elizabeth Van Lew,** a Union sympathizer who lives inside the Confederacy, begins to send information about the Southern war effort to Northern officers.

February 13, 1866: **Jesse James** and the James-Younger Gang rob the Clay County Savings and Loan Bank in Liberty, Missouri.

April 5, 1866: **Bill Miner** enters San Quentin penitentiary after being convicted of armed robbery. He is released after serving a little more than four years of his sentence.

January 23, 1871: **Bill Miner** and two accomplices rob a California stagecoach using stolen guns. He returns to San Quentin the following June.

October 9, 1871: Swindler **Sophie Lyons** is convicted of grand larceny and sentenced to serve time in Sing Sing prison.

December 19, 1872: **Sophie Lyons** escapes from Sing Sing prison using a forged key.

1873: The James-Younger Gang commits its first train robbery.

1874: Gunslinger **Clay Allison** commits his first recorded killing.

July 26, 1875: Charles Boles—better known as **Black Bart**—commits the first in a series of stagecoach robberies near Copperopolis, California.

August 3, 1877: **Black Bart** robs his fourth stagecoach, leaving behind a poem signed "Black Bart, the PO 8 [poet]."

1878: Martha Jane Cannary—known as **Calamity Jane**—acts as a nurse during a smallpox epidemic in Deadwood, Dakota Territory.

1861–65: American Civil War

1868: The Fourteenth Amendment to the Constitution of the United States is adopted

| 1850 | 1855 | 1860 | 1865 |

Spring 1878: Sam Bass and his gang stage four train holdups around Dallas, Texas.

April 1, 1878: William Bonney—also known as **Billy the Kid**—participates in an ambush that kills Sheriff William Brady in Lincoln County, New Mexico.

July 15, 1878: Texas Rangers wound and capture robber **Sam Bass** in Round Rock, Texas.

1879: Bartholomew "Bat" Masterson is appointed deputy U.S. marshal.

October 7, 1879: The second James Gang robs a train near Glendale, Missouri, of $35,000.

December 1879: Wyatt Earp arrives in lawless Tombstone, Arizona, and is soon joined by brothers James, Morgan, Virgil, and Warren.

July 14, 1880: Bill Miner is released from San Quentin prison after serving nine years for stagecoach robbery. He returns to the California prison the following year.

April 11, 1881: Dallas Stoudenmire becomes marshal of El Paso, Texas.

May 13, 1881: Convicted of murder, **Billy the Kid** is sentenced to hang.

May 25, 1881: Livestock rustler **Curly Bill,** otherwise known as William Brocius, is shot in the mouth during an argument with lawman William Breakenridge.

July 14, 1881: Sheriff Pat Garrett shoots and kills **Billy the Kid.**

October 26, 1881: Wyatt Earp and brothers Morgan and Virgil, joined by Doc Holliday, confront the Clantons and McLauries at the O.K. Corral. The gunfight leaves three men dead.

1877:
Thomas Edison is awarded the patent for the phonograph

1880:
The Metropolitan Museum of Art opens in New York City

| 1870 | 1873 | 1876 | 1879 |

April 3, 1882: Jesse James dies in St. Joseph, Missouri, after fellow outlaw Robert Ford shoots him in the back of the head.

June 1882: Pressured by city officials, **Dallas Stoudenmire** resigns from his post as marshal of El Paso.

September 18, 1882: Dallas Stoudenmire is shot and killed during a saloon brawl.

1883: Belle Starr is the first woman ever to be tried for a major crime in Judge Isaac Parker's infamous "court of the damned."

November 1883: Black Bart is captured in San Francisco, California. He pleads guilty to robbery and is sentenced to six years at San Quentin penitentiary.

October 6, 1885: Swindler **Ellen Peck** is convicted of forging a document to obtain $3,000 from the Mutual Life Insurance Company of New York. She is sentenced to four-and-a-half years in prison.

July 3, 1887: Clay Allison dies when he is run over by a freight wagon.

November 3, 1887: Robert Leroy Parker—better known as **Butch Cassidy**—and members of the McCarty Gang botch a robbery of the Denver and Rio Grande Express train in Colorado.

1889: Maverick calves stolen from the herds of Wyoming cattle barons find their way into the corral of **Cattle Kate**.

February 3, 1889: Belle Starr is ambushed and killed near her home in the Indian Territory by an unidentified gunman.

March 30, 1889: Butch Cassidy and other gang members rob the First National Bank of Denver of $20,000 in bank notes.

July 20, 1889: Cattle baron Albert J. Bothwell organizes a group to put an end to **Cattle Kate** and James Averill's cattle rustling. Watson and Averill are lynched.

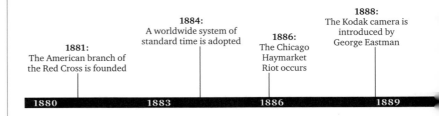

1881:
The American branch of the Red Cross is founded

1884:
A worldwide system of standard time is adopted

1886:
The Chicago Haymarket Riot occurs

1888:
The Kodak camera is introduced by George Eastman

| 1880 | 1883 | 1886 | 1889 |

1890s: Black Hand Society extortionists prey on Italian immigrants by threatening violence if their victims do not pay. The Black Hand reign of terror continues for approximately thirty years in Italian Harlem.

1890s: Swindler **Sophie Lyons** opens the New York Women's Banking and Investment Company with fellow con artist Carrie Morse. Before closing, the operation collects at least $50,000 from unsuspecting victims.

November 4, 1890: Marion Hedgepeth and other gangsters rob the Missouri Pacific train near Omaha, Nebraska. The following week they strike the Chicago, Milwaukee & St. Paul train just outside of Milwaukee, Wisconsin.

1892: After a long delay, **Marion Hedgepeth** is tried and convicted of train robbery. He is sentenced to serve twelve to twenty-five years in the state penitentiary.

1894: Posing as the wife of a Danish navy officer, **Ellen Peck** collects more than $50,000 from various banks.

July 4, 1894: Butch Cassidy is tried for cattle rustling. He is convicted and imprisoned.

July 28, 1895: Five young men, known as the **Buck Gang,** begin a murderous thirteen-day crime spree in the Indian Territory to the west of Arkansas.

August 10, 1895: All five members of the **Buck Gang** are captured and taken into custody.

1896: Calamity Jane works for an amusement company in Minneapolis, Minnesota, dressed as an army scout.

January 19, 1896: Butch Cassidy is released from the Wyoming State Penitentiary.

July 1, 1896: Rufus Buck and four other **Buck Gang** members are executed in a mass hanging at Fort Smith, Arkansas.

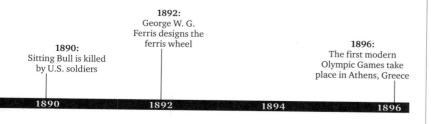

1890:
Sitting Bull is killed by U.S. soldiers

1892:
George W. G. Ferris designs the ferris wheel

1896:
The first modern Olympic Games take place in Athens, Greece

1890   1892   1894   1896

1897: Cassie Chadwick is released from prison after serving three years for fraud. She soon begins to swindle banks by claiming to be the illegitimate daughter of millionaire Andrew Carnegie.

1899: Pearl Hart and Joe Boot rob the Globe stage in the Arizona Territory—in what is recognized as the last American stagecoach robbery.

1900: When Mads Albert Sorenson dies in Chicago, his wife, **Belle Gunness,** is suspected of foul play.

May 1900: Found living in a brothel, **Calamity Jane** travels to Buffalo, New York, where she takes a job performing in a Western show at the Pan-American Exposition.

September 25, 1900: Union spy **Elizabeth Van Lew** dies in Richmond, Virginia, at the age of seventy-two.

July 3, 1901: Butch Cassidy and the Wild Bunch raid the Great Northern Flyer train near Wagner, Montana. It is the gang's final heist.

December 19, 1902: Pearl Hart leaves Yuma prison following an eighteen-month imprisonment.

August 1, 1903: Ravaged by alcoholism, **Calamity Jane** dies near Deadwood, Dakota Territory.

September 13, 1904: Bill Miner and others rob an express train outside of Vancouver, Canada.

December 7, 1904: Swindler **Cassie Chadwick** is arrested in New York. She is later convicted of six counts of fraud and sentenced to ten years in the Ohio State Penitentiary.

1905: Wealthy Brooklyn, New York, butcher Gaetano Costa refuses to pay a **Black Hand** extortionist and is shot to death in his shop.

1898:
The Spanish-American War begins

1902:
Cuba achieves independence

1903:
The Hay-Bunau-Varilla Treaty is negotiated, giving the U.S. control of the Panama Canal

1898   1900   1902   1904

1906: Cassie Chadwick dies at the age of forty-eight in the prison hospital at Ohio State Penitentiary.

1906: Belle Gunness begins to place personal ads in newspapers in Chicago and other cities in the Midwest to lure wealthy men to her Indiana farm.

1908: Joseph Weil works with Fred "the Deacon" Buckminster to trick clients into paying to have them paint buildings with a phony waterproofing substance. It is the first in a series of scams committed by Weil over the next twenty-five years.

April 28, 1908: After the farmhouse belonging to **Belle Gunness** burns to the ground, authorities discover the decapitated corpse of a woman in the ruins.

May 22, 1908: Ray Lamphere, **Belle Gunness**'s farmhand, is tried and acquitted of murder. Convicted of arson, he is sentenced to up to twenty years in prison.

1910: The six **Genna brothers**—later known as "the Terrible Gennas"—arrive in the United States from Marsala, Sicily.

January 1, 1910: Former train robber **Marion Hedgepeth** is killed by a policeman during an attempted saloon robbery.

February 22, 1911: Bill Miner commits his last train robbery at Sulfur Springs, Georgia, at the age of sixty-four.

1912: Mexican General Victoriano Huerta condemns soldier **Pancho Villa** to death. A stay of execution is later issued.

1912: The **Genna brothers** become involved in **Black Hand Society** activities in Chicago.

November 6, 1912: Eleven members of New York's Hudson Dusters Gang ambush rival gangster **Owney Madden** at a Manhattan dance hall. Left for dead, Madden lives.

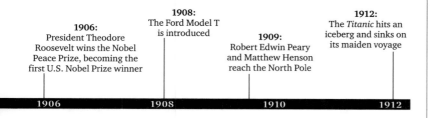

1906:
President Theodore Roosevelt wins the Nobel Peace Prize, becoming the first U.S. Nobel Prize winner

1908:
The Ford Model T is introduced

1909:
Robert Edwin Peary and Matthew Henson reach the North Pole

1912:
The *Titanic* hits an iceberg and sinks on its maiden voyage

1906   1908   1910   1912

1913: Forty-one-year-old **Diamond Joe Esposito** spends $65,000 to celebrate his marriage to sixteen-year old Carmela Marchese.

1913: *Why Crime Does Not Pay,* the autobiography of veteran swindler **Sophie Lyons,** is published.

September 2, 1913: Veteran stagecoach and train robber **Bill Miner** dies in a prison hospital in Georgia.

November 28, 1914: Owney Madden kills rival New York gangster Patsy Doyle. Sentenced to twenty years for the murder, he is released after serving nine years.

March 9, 1916: Pancho Villa and a gang of Villistas (followers of Villa) attack a small New Mexico border town and military camp, killing seventeen Americans.

1917: The obituary of stagecoach robber **Black Bart** appears in New York newspapers. Some people suspect that the death notice is a hoax engineered by the outlaw.

May 24, 1918: Bugs Moran is convicted of armed robbery and sentenced to serve time at Joliet State Prison in Illinois.

November 24, 1918: Bank robbers **Margie Dean** and husband Dale Jones are shot to death in their car by police near Los Angeles, California.

1919: Racketeer **Arnold Rothstein** masterminds the "Black Sox scandal"—the fixing of the 1919 World Series.

1919: Al Capone, a gunman for New York's notorious James Street Gang, moves to Chicago to escape arrest on a murder charge.

December 1919: Swindler **Charles Ponzi** launches an eight-month get-rich-quick scam using international postal reply coupons.

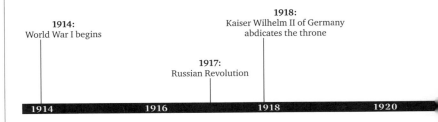

1914:
World War I begins

1917:
Russian Revolution

1918:
Kaiser Wilhelm II of Germany
abdicates the throne

1914   1916   1918   1920

1920: A grand jury meets in Chicago to investigate the 1919 Black Sox scandal.

1920: The **Genna brothers** turn Chicago's Little Italy into a vast moonshine operation.

May 8, 1924: Former swindler **Sophie Lyons** is attacked in her home. She dies later that evening in Grace Hospital in Detroit.

September 6, 1924: John Dillinger and Edgar Singleton rob an Indiana grocer, for which Dillinger is later sentenced to ten to twenty years in prison.

November 10, 1924: Chicago gangster Charles Dion O'Banion is assassinated in his North Side flower shop.

1925: Charles Ponzi is released from prison after serving four years in a Plymouth, Massachusetts, prison for mail fraud.

January 12, 1925: O'Banion gangsters attempt to ambush **Al Capone** by firing into the gangster's limousine. Capone is not injured.

January 24, 1925: Johnny Torrio, who rules Chicago's South Side bootlegging empire with **Al Capone,** is ambushed by rival gangsters.

June 13, 1925: A car filled with Genna gunmen ambushes **Bugs Moran** and Vincent "the Schemer" Drucci on Michigan Avenue in downtown Chicago. Both are wounded—but not killed.

September 20, 1926: Chicago gangster **Hymie Weiss** leads a squad of North Side gangsters in an attempt to ambush **Al Capone** at the Hawthorne Inn, the gangster's Cicero headquarters. Although more than one thousand bullets rip into the building, Capone escapes without injury.

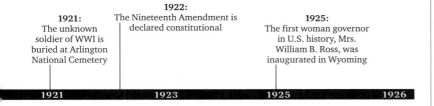

1921:
The unknown soldier of WWI is buried at Arlington National Cemetery

1922:
The Nineteenth Amendment is declared constitutional

1925:
The first woman governor in U.S. history, Mrs. William B. Ross, was inaugurated in Wyoming

| 1921 | 1923 | 1925 | 1926 |

1927: Wanted in connection with a robbery, **Ma Barker**'s boy, Herman, commits suicide during a battle with police in Wichita, Kansas.

1928: The **Purple Gang** trial ends the Cleaners and Dyers War in Detroit.

March 21, 1928: Joe Esposito dies near his Chicago home when machine-gunners fire on him from a car. Esposito is struck by fifty-eight bullets.

November 4, 1928: Racketeer **Arnold Rothstein** is shot at the Park Central Hotel in New York. He dies two days later.

1929: Twenty-year old **Irene Schroeder** abandons her husband to run away with Walter Glenn Dague. The couple soon rob a number of stores and small banks.

January 13, 1929: Former lawman **Wyatt Earp** dies in California at the age of eighty, having outlived his four brothers.

February 14, 1929: Members of **Al Capone**'s gang masquerade as policemen raiding a garage on North Clark Street in Chicago. The St. Valentine's Day Massacre leaves seven people dead.

June 13, 1929: Legs Diamond and his enforcer, Charles Entratta, kill two men at the Hotsy Totsy Club, a Manhattan speakeasy.

1930s: Meyer Lansky, Lucky Luciano, and others work together to help solidify a nationwide crime syndicate. Many former bootleggers and members of gangs such as Detroit's **Purple Gang** join the national syndicate.

November 17, 1930: Sam Battaglia robs Mrs. William Hale Thompson—the wife of the governor of Illinois—of more than $15,000 in jewels.

1927:
The first talking motion picture, *The Jazz Singer,* is released

1928:
Walt Disney introduces Mickey Mouse to the world

1929:
Great Depression begins

| 1927 | 1928 | 1929 | 1930 |

1931: Veteran gangster Joe "the Boss" Maseria is assassinated in a restaurant in Coney Island, New York. **Bugsy Siegel** is among the hitmen.

February 23, 1931: Irene Schroeder is executed at Rockview penitentiary in Pennsylvania. Her partner, Walter Glenn Dague, is executed a few days later.

April 1931: Legs Diamond is shot several times in a drive-by ambush. He survives.

June 1931: Federal officials charge Chicago gangster **Al Capone** with income tax evasion.

September 16, 1931: Three unarmed men are shot to death by **Purple Gang** mobsters. The incident is known as the Collingwood Manor Massacre.

October 1931: Al Capone is convicted of income tax evasion and sentenced to eleven years in prison.

December 17, 1931: Legs Diamond is shot dead by rival gangsters in his hotel room in Albany, New York.

1932: Gangster **Owney Madden** is released from Sing Sing prison. Later that year he is jailed again for parole violation. Released, he retires from the New York underworld.

February 2, 1932: Clyde Barrow is paroled from Eastham prison farm in Ohio—vowing that he will die before returning to prison. Barrow rejoins **Bonnie Parker** and the two embark on a two-year crime spree.

February 8, 1932: Dutch Schultz's gunmen murder Vincent Coll as Coll makes a call from a phone booth.

1931:
The *Star-Spangled Banner* becomes the national anthem of the United States

1932:
Amelia Earhart becomes the first woman to cross the Atlantic in a solo flight

1931   1932

1933: FBI agent Melvin Purvis arrests Chicago gangster **Roger Touhy** for the kidnapping of millionaire William A. Hamm, Jr. Touhy is cleared of the kidnapping, which was engineered by members of the Barker-Karpis Gang.

1933: Murder, Inc.—an enforcement division of the national crime syndicate—is formed under the leadership of **Louis Lepke.**

May 22, 1933: Thanks in part to a petition by friends and relatives, **John Dillinger** is released early from the Michigan City prison in Indiana.

July 22, 1933: Machine Gun Kelly and Albert Bates kidnap oil millionaire Charles F. Urschel from his Oklahoma City mansion.

September 26, 1933: Memphis, Tennessee, police detectives capture kidnappers **Machine Gun Kelly** and Albert Bates.

September 26, 1933: Using guns smuggled by **John Dillinger,** ten prisoners escape from the Michigan City penitentiary in Indiana. Bank robber Harry Pierpont is among the escaped convicts.

1934: Swindler **Charles Ponzi** is deported to Italy as an undesirable alien.

January 1934: The Dillinger Gang falls apart when police arrest **John Dillinger** and others in Tucson, Arizona. Dillinger is extradited to Indiana.

May 23, 1934: Bonnie and Clyde are killed by lawmen as they drive down a back road near Arcadia, Louisiana.

July 22, 1934: Tipped off by the "Lady in Red," FBI agents apprehend **John Dillinger** as he leaves Chicago's Biograph Theater. The gangster, who is recognized as Public Enemy Number One, is shot dead.

1933:
The Twenty-first
Amendment ends
Prohibition

1934:
American child
star Shirley
Temple makes
her first movie

1933   1934

1935: Two Gun Alterie is called as a government witness in the income tax evasion trial of Ralph "Bottles" Capone (brother of **Al Capone**).

1935: New York mayor Fiorello LaGuardia and district attorney Thomas E. Dewey join forces to destroy **Dutch Schultz**'s slot machine empire. Schultz later vows to kill Dewey.

1935: Ray Hamilton, a former associate of outlaws **Bonnie and Clyde,** is put to death in the electric chair.

January 8, 1935: Arthur "Doc" Barker, wanted for killing a night watchman, is captured in Chicago by FBI agent Melvin Purvis.

January 16, 1935: After a four-hour gun battle, **Ma Barker** and her son Fred are killed by lawmen near Lake Weir, Florida.

July 18, 1935: Former bootlegger **Two Gun Alterie** is killed in a machine-gun ambush.

October 23, 1935: Dutch Schultz, a member of the board of the national crime syndicate, is ambushed in a Newark, New Jersey, chophouse with three associates.

1936: Juliet Stuart Poyntz, an American communist and Soviet spy, is seen in Moscow in the company of fellow American and convicted spy George Mink.

May 1936: Alvin Karpis, a member of the Barker-Karpis Gang, is captured in New Orleans, Louisiana. FBI director J. Edgar Hoover personally places him under arrest.

1939: Gangster **Frank Costello** is tried in New Orleans, Louisiana, on charges of tax evasion. The government loses its case because of lack of evidence.

August 24, 1939: Racketeer **Louis Lepke** surrenders to the FBI through newspaper columnist Walter Winchell.

1935:
The Social Security Act is signed by President Franklin D. Roosevelt

1936:
Spanish Civil War begins

1939:
World War II begins

1935   1936   1937   1938

1940: Joseph Weil is sentenced to three years in prison for a mail-fraud charge involving phony oil leases. It is the veteran swindler's final conviction.

October 9, 1942: Roger Touhy and six other prisoners escape from Joliet penitentiary. The escaped convicts are soon placed on the FBI's Most Wanted list.

December 1942: FBI agents capture **Roger Touhy** at a boardinghouse in Chicago.

1943: American Communist Party member **Julius Rosenberg** is recruited by KGB agent Aleksander Feklisov to spy for the Soviet Union.

March 4, 1944: Murder, Inc., chief **Louis Lepke** is executed in the electric chair at Sing Sing prison.

1945: Meyer Lansky and **Bugsy Siegel** begin to establish a gambling hotel in a small western town called Las Vegas, Nevada.

June 1945: Julius Rosenberg arranges for his brother-in-law, David Greenglass, to provide a courier with classified information about the A-bomb.

December 1946: At a gangster summit in Havana, Cuba, **Bugsy Siegel** swears to fellow syndicate members that he has not stolen mob money through his Las Vegas gambling operation.

January 25, 1947: Retired gangster **Al Capone** dies at his mansion in Palm Island, Florida.

June 20, 1947: Bugsy Siegel is shot to death in the living room of **Virginia Hill**'s Beverly Hills mansion.

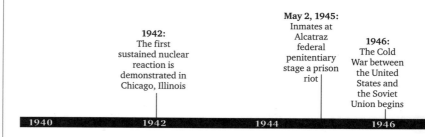

1942:
The first sustained nuclear reaction is demonstrated in Chicago, Illinois

May 2, 1945:
Inmates at Alcatraz federal penitentiary stage a prison riot

1946:
The Cold War between the United States and the Soviet Union begins

1940   1942   1944   1946

1949: Lloyd Barker, the only surviving member of the Barker Gang, is shot to death by his wife.

January 1949: Charles Ponzi dies in the charity ward of a Brazilian hospital at the age of sixty-six.

1950s: Working under **Sam Giancana, Sam Battaglia** becomes chief of the Chicago Outfit's narcotics operations.

May 10, 1950: The Senate Special Committee to Investigate Organized Crime in Interstate Commerce, spearheaded by Senator Estes Kefauver, subpoenas the testimony of numerous gangsters in a year-long attempt to piece together an accurate picture of organized crime in America.

June 15, 1950: Questioned by the FBI, David Greenglass implicates his sister, **Ethel Rosenberg,** and her husband, **Julius,** in espionage.

May 1951: "Queen of the Mob" **Virginia Hill** appears as a key witness before the Kefauver Committee and shocks committee members with her candid responses.

March 6, 1951: Ethel and Julius Rosenberg are tried for conspiracy to commit espionage.

June 19, 1953: In spite of worldwide pleas for clemency, **Ethel and Julius Rosenberg** are electrocuted at Sing Sing prison.

1954: Bank robber and kidnapper **Machine Gun Kelly** suffers a fatal heart attack in Leavenworth prison.

June 23, 1954: A federal grand jury charges **Virginia Hill** with income tax evasion.

1956: Retired swindler **Joseph Weil** is called to testify before a Senate subcommittee, led by Senator Estes Kefauver, investigating juvenile delinquency.

1950:
Korean War
begins

1953:
The first
atomic
artillery
shell is fired

1954:
Racial
segregation in
public schools
is declared
unconstitutional

1948   1950   1952   1954

1957: Bugs Moran dies from cancer in Leavenworth penitentiary, where he is serving time for bank robbery.

October 25, 1957: Mobster Albert Anastasia is shot to death in the barber shop of the Park Sheraton Hotel in New York City. Rival gangsters **Carlo Gambino** and Vito Genovese are believed to be responsible for ordering the murder.

1959: FBI agents plant a microphone in the backroom of the Forest Park, Illinois, headquarters of mobster **Sam Giancana.**

November 25, 1959: Convicted kidnapper **Roger Touhy** is released from prison after the kidnapping he was found guilty of is revealed to have been a hoax.

December 17, 1959: Former bootlegger **Roger Touhy** is gunned down near his sister's Chicago home.

1960s: The U.S. government begins to subpoena gangster **Carlo Gambino** to appear before the grand jury to investigate his decades-long involvement in organized crime.

1965: After refusing to testify about the mob's activities before a federal grand jury in Chicago, mobster **Sam Giancana** is sentenced to one year in prison.

March 25, 1966: Virginia Hill dies from an overdose of sleeping pills near Salzburg, Austria.

December 1969: Diana Oughton, a former social activist, attends a secret meeting of the Weathermen, a terrorist organization, in Flint, Michigan.

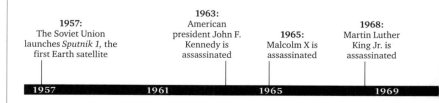

1957:
The Soviet Union launches *Sputnik 1,* the first Earth satellite

1963:
American president John F. Kennedy is assassinated

1965:
Malcolm X is assassinated

1968:
Martin Luther King Jr. is assassinated

| 1957 | 1961 | 1965 | 1969 |

1970: JoAnne Chesimard—also known as Assata Shakur—joins the Black Panther Party.

March 1970: Diana Oughton dies as a bomb explodes in a house in New York City. The house is a bomb factory for Weathermen terrorists.

March 23, 1971: Author **Clifford Irving** signs a contract with McGraw-Hill publishing company to write an authorized biography of billionaire Howard Hughes, who has not been interviewed by journalists since 1958.

November 1971: D. B. Cooper hijacks Northwest Airlines flight 305.

December 1971: Employees of **Jerry Schneider** inform officials at the Pacific Telephone & Telegraph company in Los Angeles, California, that their boss is using access to the phone company's computerized inventory system to order products illegally.

February 1972: Investigators for the Los Angeles District Attorney obtain a search warrant for the business of **Jerry Schneider.** Schneider is later charged with receiving stolen property and sentenced to two months in prison.

March 9, 1972: Author **Clifford Irving** is charged with federal conspiracy to defraud, forgery, and several other charges for writing the fake autobiography of Howard Hughes.

1973: Mobster **Sam Battaglia** dies in prison, having served six years of a fifteen-year sentence for extortion.

February 18, 1973: Retired mobster **Frank Costello** dies of natural causes at the age of eighty-two.

July 4, 1973: "To my people"—a speech in which **JoAnne Chesimard** describes herself as a black revolutionary—is publicly broadcast.

1972:
The Watergate affair—the burglary of Democratic headquarters in Washington, D.C., takes place

1973:
Skylab, the first U.S. space station, is launched

| 1970 | 1971 | 1972 | 1973 |

1974: JoAnne Chesimard and fellow Black Liberation Army member Fred Hilton are tried and acquitted of a 1972 bank robbery in New York.

February 4, 1974: Newspaper heiress **Patty Hearst** is kidnapped by members of the Symbionese Liberation Army (SLA).

April 5, 1974: Patty Hearst records a message to announce publicly that she has joined the SLA.

July 29, 1974: College dropout **Christopher Boyce** begins work at TRW Systems, an aerospace firm that works on many classified military programs. The following year Boyce and friend **Andrew Daulton Lee** devise a plan to provide Soviet agents with top-secret information.

June 2, 1975: John Gotti pleads guilty to attempted manslaughter in the second degree for the murder of James McBratney in Staten Island, New York.

September 18, 1975: Patty Hearst is captured with terrorist Wendy Yoshimura in an apartment in San Francisco.

October 15, 1975: Mobster **Carlo Gambino** dies of a heart attack at his home in Long Island, New York, at the age of seventy-three.

October 10, 1976: Convicted telephone thief **Jerry Schneider** appears on a *60 Minutes* television segment called "Dial E for Embezzlement."

1977: Gordon Kahl, a member of the conservative survivalist group called Posse Comitatus, is convicted of failing to file federal income tax returns. He is placed on probation.

March 25, 1977: JoAnne Chesimard is convicted of the murder of a New Jersey state trooper. She is sentenced to life in prison plus more than twenty-five years.

April 1977: Christopher Boyce and Andrew Daulton Lee— the Falcon and the Snowman—are tried for espionage. Both are convicted.

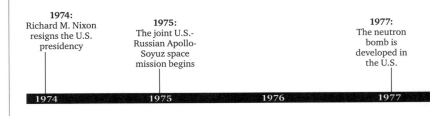

1974:
Richard M. Nixon resigns the U.S. presidency

1975:
The joint U.S.-Russian Apollo-Soyuz space mission begins

1977:
The neutron bomb is developed in the U.S.

1974   1975   1976   1977

November 5, 1978: FBI agents arrest computer thief **Stanley Rifkin** in Carlsbad, California.

January 1979: President Jimmy Carter commutes the prison sentence of convicted bank robber **Patty Hearst.**

February 13, 1979: Released on bail, computer thief **Stanley Rifkin** is arrested for initiating a wire fraud of the Union Bank of Los Angeles. A month later he is convicted of two counts of wire fraud and is sentenced to eight years in federal prison.

November 2, 1979: Convicted murderer **JoAnne Chesimard** escapes from the New Jersey Corrections Institute for women. She later flees to Cuba.

January 1980: Convicted spy **Christopher Boyce** escapes from a federal prison in Lompoc, California. Nineteen months later he is captured and returned to prison—with ninety years added to his original sentence.

April 1980: Two children discover a package containing several dozen $20 bills near Portland, Oregon. The serial numbers are traced to the ransom payment in the **D. B. Cooper** hijacking.

May 28, 1980: John Favara, the man responsible for the accidental killing of gangster **John Gotti**'s twelve-year-old son, disappears. He is never seen again.

January 15, 1983: **Meyer Lansky** dies of cancer in a New York hospital at the age of eighty-one.

February 13, 1983: Federal marshals attempt to serve tax evader **Gordon Kahl** with a warrant for violating parole. A shootout follows, in which two marshals are killed.

May 11, 1983: **Gordon Kahl** and two others are charged with the murders of two federal marshals.

June 4, 1983: **Gordon Kahl** dies in a shootout with federal marshals near Smithville, Arkansas.

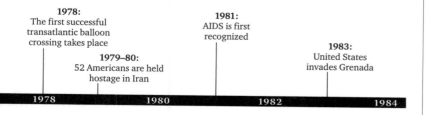

1978:
The first successful transatlantic balloon crossing takes place

1979–80:
52 Americans are held hostage in Iran

1981:
AIDS is first recognized

1983:
United States invades Grenada

1978   1980   1982   1984

April 1985: CIA agent **Aldrich Ames** begins to work as a Soviet spy.

June 2, 1986: San Francisco peace activist **Katya Komisaruk** destroys a government computer on the Vandenberg Air Force base as an anti-nuclear protest.

August 1986: Astronomer Clifford Stoll discovers a seventy-five cent shortfall in his computer system's accounting records. He later discovers that the shortfall is due to an unauthorized user who has broken into the system to access classified information without being traced.

March 13, 1987: Gangster **John Gotti** is tried on charges of racketeering. The "Teflon don" is acquitted.

November 1987: Katya Komisaruk is tried on one count of destruction of government property. During her trial, many supporters appear in court carrying white roses as a symbol of solidarity.

January 11, 1988: Convicted of destroying government property, **Katya Komisaruk** is sentenced to five years in federal prison.

March 2, 1989: Clifford Stoll's investigation of computer records leads to a spy ring of West German computer hackers. **Marcus Hess** and two others are arrested in Hanover, West Germany.

July 1989: Computer hacker **Kevin Mitnick** is sentenced to one year in federal prison at Lompoc, California, for breaking into telephone company computers and stealing long-distance access codes.

1992: John Gotti is tried and convicted of fourteen counts of racketeering and murder after being betrayed by former aide Salvatore "Sammy the Bull" Gravano.

May 12, 1993: The FBI begins a criminal investigation of **Aldrich Ames,** who is suspected of spying for the Soviets.

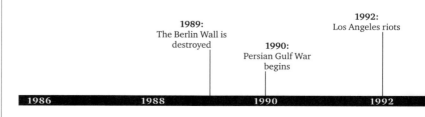

1989:
The Berlin Wall is destroyed

1990:
Persian Gulf War begins

1992:
Los Angeles riots

1986   1988   1990   1992

February 21, 1994: Soviet spy **Aldrich Ames** is arrested as he drives to work at CIA headquarters. He is later convicted of espionage and sentenced to life in prison.

December 24, 1994: Convicted hacker **Kevin Mitnick** steals data from the home computer of computer security expert Tsutomu Shimomura.

February 15, 1995: Federal agents arrest **Kevin Mitnick** in Raleigh, North Carolina, without a struggle.

April 19, 1995: A bomb explodes in front of the Alfred P. Murrah Federal Building in Oklahoma City, Oklahoma, killing 168 people. **Timothy McVeigh** is arrested a short time later.

November 21, 1996: Archaeologists find what they believe to be the long-lost flagship of **Blackbeard** the pirate.

April 1997: The trial of suspected terrorist **Timothy McVeigh** begins in Denver, Colorado.

June 2, 1997: **Timothy McVeigh** is convicted of all eleven charges against him involving the Oklahoma City bombing.

December 1997: A group of hackers break into an Internet site and leave behind a computerized ransom note threatening to release a computer virus if **Kevin Mitnick** is not set free.

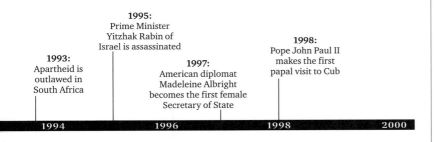

1993:
Apartheid is outlawed in South Africa

1995:
Prime Minister Yitzhak Rabin of Israel is assassinated

1997:
American diplomat Madeleine Albright becomes the first female Secretary of State

1998:
Pope John Paul II makes the first papal visit to Cub

1994   1996   1998   2000

Picture Credits

The photographs and illustrations appearing in *Outlaws, Mobsters & Crooks: From the Old West to the Internet* were received from the following sources:

On the cover: Al Capone (**Archive Photos, Inc. Reproduced by permission**).

AP/Wide World Photos, Inc. Reproduced by permission: pp. 3, 11, 18, 31, 35, 45, 50, 56, 67, 72, 80, 87, 100, 109, 110, 127, 139, 151, 156, 159, 178, 186, 190, 193, 207, 217, 220, 226, 227, 230, 241, 247, 262, 266, 269, 270, 283, 305, 310, 311, 313, 328, 336, 351, 373, 392, 394, 437, 440, 443, 451, 459, 462; **Archive Photos, Inc. Reproduced by permission:** pp. 13, 21, 89, 121, 235, 292, 378, 410, 450; **UPI/Corbis-Bettmann. Reproduced by permission:** pp. 16, 22, 28, 41, 47, 54, 55, 58, 75, 93, 96, 105, 144, 147, 164, 177, 205, 261, 278, 294, 297, 325, 430, 434, 448, 456, 465; **Photograph by Greta Pratt. New York Times Co./Archive Photos, Inc. Reproduced by permission:** p. 39; **The Granger Collection, New York. Reproduced by permission:** pp. 113, 333, 355, 367, 387, 397, 412, 419, 492; **Popperfoto/Archive Photos, Inc. Reproduced by permission:** p. 133; **Photograph by Tammy Lechner. Los Angeles Times Photo. Reproduced by permission:** p. 189; **Reuters/The News and Observer-Jim/Archive Photos, Inc. Reproduced by permission:** p. 197; **Reuters/Corbis-Bettmann. Reproduced by permission:** p. 221; **Wyoming Division of Cultural Resources. Reproduced by permission:** p. 253; **Reuters/Jim Bourg/Archive Photos. Reproduced by permission:** p. 315; **Photograph by Eric Draper. AP/Wide World Photos, Inc. Reproduced by permission:** p. 317; **American Stock/Archive Photos, Inc. Reproduced by permission:** pp. 341, 347, 368; **The Library of Congress:** p. 360; **Corbis-Bettmann. Reproduced by permission:** pp. 364, 384, 398, 486, 490; **Corbis. Reproduced by permission:** pp. 380, 477, 482.

Bandits
and Gunslingers

"**O**utlaws are made, not born," lawman Wyatt Earp once said. Was Jesse James a born bandit who was destined to rob trains? Did Billy the Kid's upbringing turn him into a killer? Would Butch Cassidy have been a crook if he'd been born in Boston? These aren't questions that can be answered. But they're questions that provide an interesting glimpse into the life and times of the bandits and gunslingers who contributed to the legend of the Wild West.

In this section you'll read all about outlaws—from legendary gunslinger Clay Allison to Pancho Villa, the Mexican revolutionary who became a hero to some and a villain to others. You'll find out about their early lives, the people they met, the circumstances they encountered—and the details involving their final days.

Clay Allison
(Robert Clay Allison)

Born: 1840 or 1841
Died: July 3, 1887

Gunslinger Clay Allison was once asked what he did for a living. "I am a shootist" was his response. Although in reality he killed fewer men than many other outlaws, he has gone down in history as one of the most infamous gunslingers in the West.

A SOUTHERN BOY

Born in the Tennessee countryside, Allison received little schooling. Almost twenty years old when the Civil War erupted in 1861, Allison served in the Confederate Army—both as a spy and as a scout for Confederate General Nathan Bedford Forrest (1821–1877). After the war ended, he headed south to Texas to find work as a cowboy. He drove cattle from Texas to Kansas and worked on ranches in Colorado and New Mexico—and trouble followed wherever he went.

During the 1870s, Allison worked for many wealthy cattle owners in the border state of New Mexico. In 1874 he committed his first killing—his first *recorded* killing, that is—when he shot a man near the Canadian River in New Mexico. Allison was probably also involved in a number of other killings that took place in Colorado, Kansas, New Mexico, and Texas around that time. He justified his killings by claiming that he was protecting property holders from thieves and murderers. And he made no

Bat Masterson 1853-1921

Bartholomew "Bat" Masterson wasn't a man to back down from a fight. A member of the infamous "Dodge City Peace Commission"—which included **Wyatt Earp** (see entry), Doc Holliday, and Charlie Bassett, among others—he was one of the most prominent lawmen in the Old West.

Masterson had deadly aim with a gun. Describing what was required to become an accurate shooter, Masterson wrote this:

To accustom his hands to the pistols of those days, the man who coveted [desired] a reputation started in early and practiced with them just as a card shark practices with his cards, as a shell game man drills his fingers to manipulate the elusive pea, or a juggler must practice to acquire proficiency [to become skilled]. When he could draw, cock and fire all in one smooth lightning-quick movement, he could then detach [remove] his mind from that movement and concentrate on accuracy.

There is no question that Masterson was a well-practiced pistol shooter. "It was not magic which enabled Bat Masterson to produce some wizard-like effects with the draw. It was hard and unrelenting practice," a journalist named Arthur Chapman wrote in the January 3, 1930, edition of the New York *Herald-Tribune*. Chapman interviewed a man named John L. Amos, who, as a young man, had been Masterson's roommate in Dodge City, Kansas. Apparently, sharing a room with the gunslinger was a nerve-racking experience. Amos told the journalist:

The only complaint I had against my roommates [Masterson and Conk Jones, another gunslinger] was that they were always practicing gunplay. For at least an hour every day, they would practice with unloaded guns, draw and click, draw and click. . . . Masterson and Conk practiced their gunplay in the room and generally, I was the target. I would hear a click behind me and would turn around to find that one of them had snapped his

apologies for his chosen occupation. He reportedly once said, "I never killed a man who didn't need it."

TALL TALES

A tall, good-looking man with brown hair and blue eyes, Allison was a drunk. Although there's no doubt that he was deadly with a gun and played a role in killing a number of men, many of the stories about his exploits are either far-fetched exaggerations—or utterly untrue. In one such story, a drunken

revolver at me. If I came in the door, perhaps both of them would go through the motion of drawing and firing at me as I entered. I liked both of them a lot, but finally I had to tell them that my nerves were going to pieces, and I would have to hand in my official resignation as their target.

Before he became a peace officer, Masterson dabbled in a number of occupations. Born in St. George, Quebec in Canada, and raised in the Midwest, he left for Kansas in 1872 with his brother, Ed, to join a railroad gang in Dodge City. After one year of railroad labor, he took work as a buffalo hunter—something many other noted gunfighters had done.

Back in Dodge City, Masterson was employed as a city policeman. In 1877, he was elected sheriff of Ford County, Kansas. Here are some of the highlights of his career:

- Captured Dave Rudabaugh and Edgar West after they attempted to rob a train near Kinsley, Kansas

- Led a posse (a group of people with legal authority to capture criminals)—which included Wyatt Earp among its ranks—that captured James W. Kennedy, who was accused in the slaying of a woman who worked in a dance-hall

- Was appointed a deputy U.S. marshal in 1879; after serving his term, Masterson was defeated for re-election

Masterson was also an avid gambler. In 1881, he moved to Tombstone in the Arizona Territory to work for Wyatt Earp as a card dealer at the Oriental Saloon. He ended his career in New York City—as a journalist. Masterson earned a favorable reputation as a writer and sports editor for the *New York Morning Telegraph,* and was recognized as an authority on prizefighting (boxing). Masterson died of a heart attack on October 25, 1921.

Allison gallops through the streets in a Texas town—wearing nothing but his boots and his hat—as he empties his guns into storefront windows. Another tale recounts an episode with a dentist who mistakenly pulled the wrong tooth. As revenge, the story goes, Allison pulled a gun on the dentist—as well as one of the dentist's teeth.

Allison apparently shot his friend-turned-enemy Chuck Colbert. In one account of the shooting, Allison and Colbert meet at a restaurant in Texas for dinner. Following a stare-down, during which the outlaws stir their coffees with the muzzles of their

Bat Masterson.

guns, Allison draws on Colbert, shooting him in the forehead. As his former friend's body is carried away, the hard-hearted shootist continues his meal—without even looking up. Francisco "Pancho" Griego, a Mexican outlaw, met a similar fate. When Allison realized that Griego was using his sombrero to hide a gun, he shot him without asking any questions.

Other stories have Allison forcing various lawmen—including Wyatt Earp and Bat Masterson—to back down. But there is no evidence to support any such meetings. In fact, Allison probably avoided face-to-face confrontations with lawmen. Ironically, Allison didn't die in a blaze of gunfire. Drunk, he fell out of a heavy freight wagon, and was killed when the wheel rolled over him. Allison's grave is in Peco, Texas.

Sources for Further Reading

The American West, A Cultural Encyclopedia, Volumes 1 and 6. Danbury, CT: Grolier Educational Corp., 1995, pp. 28–29, 968–971.

Nash, Jay Robert. *Bloodletters and Badmen.* New York: M. Evans, 1973, pp. 18–19.

Rosa, Joseph. *The Taming of the West: Age of the Gunfighter.* New York: Smithmark, 1993, pp. 120–121.

Wukovits, John. *The Gunslingers.* Broomall, PA: Chelsea House, 1997, p. 17.

Richard Barter

Born: 1834
Died: July 11, 1859
AKA: Rattlesnake Dick

A small-time outlaw, Richard Barter organized a gang of thieves that robbed a mule train carrying thousands of dollars in gold. The robbery was a success—but the gold was lost—and none of the thieves ever profited from the heist.

A GOLDEN OPPORTUNITY

The son of a British officer, Richard Barter was born in either England or Quebec, Canada. He moved to the United States when he was young. In his teens, he headed for California to pan for gold—only to find himself employed by large companies that made it difficult for an individual gold-digger to strike it rich. Barter soon turned to theft—and was soon caught. Found guilty of stealing horses, he was jailed for two years. Soon after his release, Barter, who was known as "Rattlesnake Dick," formed a gang made up of George Skinner, his brother, Cyrus Skinner, a horse thief called Big Dolph Newton, Bill Carter, who had a reputation as a fast shot, and a man named Romero. Barter first had the gang commit small robberies—as practice for a larger job he had in mind.

During the gold-rush era, thousands of dollars worth of gold bullion (gold still in raw or unrefined form) were transported out of the hills by mule trains that were accompanied by armed guards. After studying the movements of shipments in

All that glitters--the California gold rush

In 1848, Alta, California, was a modest frontier outpost with a population of about 14,000. The following year Alta's population skyrocketed and by 1850, the area's population had grown to about 100,000 residents. The reason for the population explosion: gold fever.

John Augustus Sutter, a German-born Swiss immigrant, created a 50,000-acre agricultural empire in northern California. On his lands were orchards, fields, and a fort (manned with an army). In January 1848, his foreman—James Wilson Marshall, a thirty-eight-year-old carpenter from New Jersey—had instructions to build a sawmill on Sutter's property, at a bend of the South Fork of the American River. As his crew deepened the millrace (a canal in which water flows to and from a mill wheel), Marshall spotted something shiny. He later recalled, "My eye was caught by something shining in the bottom of the ditch . . . I reached my hand down and picked it up; it made my heart thump, for I was certain it was gold."

Indeed it was. Marshall brought the nugget back to Sutter's Fort, where he and his employer tested it—according to methods outlined in an encyclopedia. Although Sutter tried to keep the discovery secret, word soon spread through California and beyond. On March 18, 1848, a San Francisco newspaper announced "Gold Mine Found." Sometime later a young Mormon named Sam Brannan stirred up public interest when he marched through the streets of San Francisco with a bottle filled with gold dust shouting, "Gold! Gold! Gold from the American River!" Within one month, thousands of men abandoned San Francisco in hopes of striking it rich in the gold fields. News of the bonanza hit New York before summer—when it was announced in the *New York Herald*.

In 1849, the peak year of the California Gold Rush, about 80,000 "Forty-niners" (the name refers to the year the California Gold Rush

Wet gold claims

Miners in California worked gold claims that stretched over 400 miles of rivers and streams including the American, Feather, Mercedes, Stanislaus, and Yuba.

the area, Barter came up with a plan to steal a fortune in gold by stopping the Wells Fargo mule team that carried bullion out of the Trinity Mountains. He sent his men to ambush the mule train—but he didn't join them.

BURIED TREASURE

Barter's plan was a success. The gang members headed down the mountain pass with $80,000 worth of gold—an enormous amount of money in that day. But what Barter hadn't real-

began) arrived in California. Nine-tenths of the miners were men—and more than half of them were under twenty years old. Most of them had been tradesmen or farmers before taking up the shovel and pan. Some were military men. Infected by gold fever, soldiers deserted their posts and sailors jumped ship. The majority of miners were from the United States—two-thirds of whom came from the eastern states of New England. Many of the Forty-niners were foreign-born. Mining camps became a melting pot of Chinese, Mexicans, Irish, Russians, West Indians, Italians, French, and Australians.

Life in the dismal mining towns was expensive. Forced to pay outrageous prices for food and supplies (the price of a common shovel was reported to have increased by 800 percent), the miners lived in squalid (poverty-ridden) conditions. In a letter home, one miner reported, "You can scarcely form any conception of what a dirty business this gold digging is and of the mode of life which a miner is compelled to lead. We all live more like brutes than humans." Not surpris-

ingly, violence was a problem in mining regions: miners were stoned to death in arguments over gambling, well-armed claim stakers readily shot intruders, and dead bodies were sometimes seen floating down rivers. Historians estimate that the homicide rate in the mining frontier was several times higher than it is in today's major American cities.

The work was back-breaking. Eroded (worn away) into dust, nuggets and flakes, the gold combined with sand and gravel in the bottom of stream beds. In order to sift the gold from worthless sludge, miners had to "wash" the contents of streambeds. They used a variety of methods. Gold panning entailed shoveling sand and gravel into a rocker or cradle. Some used a sluice (a long trough) called a "Long Tom" that allowed them to wash greater quantities. During the peak years of the gold rush, gold sold for $15 to $16 an ounce. Although some miners struck it rich, the odds were poor: it is estimated that only one out of every one hundred miners earned more than $16 a day.

ized was that the mules—which were clearly marked with the Wells Fargo brand—would not be able to complete the difficult trip out of the mountains. Somewhere near Ureka, the three robbers were forced to abandon what they couldn't carry. They buried most of their haul.

Barter and Cyrus Skinner were supposed to meet the rest of the gang at Folsom to divide the gold. But before they were able to rejoin their accomplices, they were thrown in jail for stealing mules. Since lawmen didn't suspect them of being involved in the gold robbery, their sentence was short. Meanwhile, posses

That's a lot of money!

It is estimated that between 1848 and 1857, $500 million in gold was mined in California.

Hidden treasure

No one has ever found the gold that Barter's partner, George Skinner, buried after the Wells Fargo mule train holdup. To this day, a fortune in gold is buried somewhere in the foothills of the Trinity Mountains in California.

(groups of people summoned by a sheriff to aid in law enforcement) of lawmen and Wells Fargo detectives had been hunting the countryside for the thieves who robbed the mule train. When the lawmen found the thieves, a shoot-out erupted. George Skinner was killed and Romero was severely wounded. Newton and Carter surrendered. While Carter gave up the remaining gold in exchange for his freedom, Romero and Newton were sent to prison.

After they were released from jail, Barter and Cyrus Skinner searched the foothills for the buried gold. They found nothing. Having earned nothing from the gold heist, they turned to stagecoach robbery and were soon pursued by local lawmen. On July 11, 1859, Barter encountered Sheriff J. Boggs, who shot and killed him with a single bullet. He was twenty-five years old. Skinner was wounded and later sentenced to a lengthy imprisonment.

Sources for Further Reading

The American West, A Cultural Encyclopedia, Volume 4. Danbury, CT: Grolier Educational Corp., 1995, pp. 634–636.

Courtrigt, David T. "Violence in America." *American Heritage* (September 1996), p. 36+.

Louis, Ted. "Hidden California Gold Treasure." *Stamps* (January 7, 1995), p. 12.

Nash, Jay Robert. *Bloodletters and Badmen.* New York: M. Evans, 1973, p. 46.

Nash, Jay Robert. *The Encyclopedia of Western Lawmen and Outlaws.* New York: DaCapo, 1994, p. 25.

Nash, Jay Robert. *The Encyclopedia of World Crime.* Wilmette, IL: Crime Books, 1990, p. 265.

Ward, Geoffrey. *The West, An Illustrated History.* Boston: Little, Brown, 1996, pp. 120–165.

Sam Bass

Born: July 21, 1851
Died: July 21, 1878

"Sam Bass was not much of an outlaw as outlaws go. He was no gunman, nor was he a killer," wrote Charles L. Martin in A Sketch of Sam Bass, the Bandit. But somehow, he was transformed into a folk hero even before he was betrayed by a gang member.

A ROUGH CHILDHOOD

One of ten children, Sam Bass was born in Indiana on July 21, 1851. Two of his siblings died as infants, and one of his brothers was killed fighting as a member of the Sixteenth Indiana Regiment during the Civil War (1861–1865). His mother, Elizabeth Sheeks Bass, died at the age of thirty-nine, shortly after her tenth child was born. Sam was just ten years old at the time.

Sam's father, Daniel Bass, married a woman who had two children from an earlier marriage. Together the couple had a son. Shortly thereafter, on February 20, 1864, Daniel died of pneumonia. He was forty-two. Having sold the family farm, Sam's stepmother was forced to send the children to live with relatives. Twelve-year-old Sam went with two of his brothers and three of his sisters to live with an uncle, David Sheeks.

Sam's uncle put the children to work on his farm. Sam plowed, hoed corn and potatoes, harvested, butchered, and sheered sheep. He rarely went to school and he never learned to read and write. And he soon grew tired of working for no pay on his uncle's farm.

FAST PONIES AND CATTLE SCAMS

At the age of eighteen, Bass ran away. He left with no money and only the clothes on his back. Taking odd jobs to support himself, he made his way west, where he hoped to become a cowboy. In Denton, in northeastern Texas, he worked as a hired hand for the sheriff, W. F. "Dad" Egan.

Horse racing was a popular pastime in Denton. Bass enjoyed betting at the race track and eventually purchased a horse—Jenny, a mare (female horse)—with the sheriff's younger brother. Egan didn't approve of the people who were associated with horse racing, and offered to lend Bass the money to buy out his brother's share in the mare.

Bass eventually quit his job and devoted his time to horse racing. He traveled through southwest Texas, the Indian territories, and Mexico with his friend, Henry Underwood, to enter his horse in races. Jenny—who became known as "the Denton Mare"—won most of the races she ran in.

Bass started out as a hard-working, honest young man who handled his money well. But he soon began to gamble at cards and drink heavily. On a trip to San Antonio, Texas, he made friends with Joel Collins, a former cowboy who owned a bar in town. Collins had been tried and acquitted in 1870 for murdering a man named Bedal Rosalees. Soon after meeting Bass, Collins sold his bar, and the two came up with a scheme to use the Denton Mare to win even more money.

Collins posed as the owner of the Denton Mare, while Bass pretended to be a horse trainer. After he hired on to work for another man who owned a race horse, Bass would test the horse to see if it was capable of beating the Denton Mare. If he thought the mare could beat the other horse, Bass encouraged the owner to enter the horse in a race against the Denton Mare. He also urged the owner to bet heavily on his horse. The Denton Mare always won—earning Bass and Collins easy money.

Bass and Collins eventually sold the Denton Mare. In the summer of 1876 they bought several hundred cattle in order to make money trail-herding them to Kansas. Since they didn't have enough cash to pay for the entire herd, they left for Kansas heavily in debt. North of Dodge City, Kansas, Bass and Collins sold the cattle. They made a handsome profit and could easily have repaid their debt. Instead, they kept all the money, and headed for Deadwood, in the Black Hills of the Dakota Territory. There, they gambled and made poor investments. In no time they lost all their earnings.

Grave words

Bass's grave marker was simple but to the point:

Samuel Bass

Born July 21st 1851

Died July 21st 1878

A Brave Man Reposes in Death Here.

Why Was He Not True?

EASY MONEY

Bass and Collins decided to try their luck at stagecoach robbery. They formed a gang with three other men, and tried to stop the Deadwood Stage, which was carrying $15,000. When they yelled, "Halt!" the driver tried to stop—but the horses were scared and continued to run. One of the robbers shot the driver, killing him.

Hunted as wanted outlaws, Bass and Collins attempted a few more stagecoach robberies, with little success. One robbery yielded as little as $3. Next they turned to train robbery, which turned out to be much more rewarding. Joining with four other outlaws, they planned to rob an express train that had departed from San Francisco with a Wells Cargo freight car. After consulting the railroad's timetable, they met the train at Big Springs, Nebraska, and stopped it as it labored uphill. The robbers never managed to break into the safe, which contained about $200,000. But they did ride off with $60,000 in $20 gold pieces that had been stored in wooden boxes—and about $1,300 in loot taken from passengers.

Wells Fargo offered a reward for their capture. Dozens of railroad detectives and posses (groups of people with legal authority to capture criminals) soon hounded the robbers as they tried to make their way back to Texas. To throw their pursuers off their trail, the outlaws split into pairs. Bass went with Jack Davis, while Collins rode with a man who called

Copycat robber

As a boy, Sam Bass heard stories about the daring train robberies committed by the Reno brothers, who lived about forty miles from his family's farm. The Reno brothers are credited with committing the first American train robbery. Long after most of them had been hanged, Bass employed their methods for holding up trains.

Bullet graffiti

Although evidence suggests that he never killed anyone, Sam Bass had a reputation as a deadly accurate shooter. According to one story, the outlaw shot his initials into an oak tree without even pausing to steady his aim.

himself Bill Heffridge. Collins and Heffridge were both killed in a shoot-out with soldiers. Davis disappeared, never to be heard from again. Another gang member, Tom Nixon, also vanished—even though the Pinkerton Detective Agency was conducting a nation-wide manhunt for the outlaws. Bass managed to make it back to Denton, Texas, where he organized another band of outlaws.

GROWING SUSPICION

After committing a few moderately successful stagecoach robberies, Bass decided that it was time to return to train robbery. He organized a gang that included his friend, Henry Underwood, and some new recruits: Frank Jackson, Seaborn Barnes—who had been acquitted of a shooting when he was seventeen years old—and Tom Spotswood. In the spring of 1878, Bass and his gang staged four train holdups around Dallas.

Alarmed by the robbers' repeated offenses, the governor of Texas called out the Texas Rangers. Pinkerton Detectives from Chicago joined the manhunt, as did a number of other law officers. But none of them was able to capture Bass, who hid for some time in Cove Hollow—a steep, hilly area near Denton. Many of the local people defended Bass, while others began to suspect that he was one of the outlaws who had robbed the Big Springs train. Each of the stolen $20 gold pieces—which were called double eagles—had the same date, 1877. Sam Bass had been going around town for some time spending $20 double eagles stamped with that date.

A TRAITOR IN THE GANG

Bass never managed to match the success of the first train robbery at Big Springs. Hungry for some quick cash, he decided to try his hand at bank robbery. Together with his bandit recruits, he planned to rob a bank in Round Rock, Texas. One of the new members of Bass's gang was Jim Murphy, whose family had hidden Bass after one of his train robberies.

Goodnight little doggies

Shortly after Sam Bass was killed, a ballad that described his life and betrayal appeared. The song was a favorite among cowboys on the range, who sang it as they rode slowly around their cattle at night. The final four verses below describe Sam's betrayal at the hands of Jim Murphy, the gang-member-turned-traitor:

Jim Murphy was arrested and then
   released on bail;
He jumped his bond at Tyler and took the
   train for Terrell.
But Major Jones had posted Jim and that
   was all a stall;
'Twas only a plan to capture Sam before
   the coming fall.

Sam met his fate at Round Rock, July the
   twenty-first;
They pierced poor Sam with rifle balls and
   emptied out his purse.

Poor Sam he is a corpse and six foot under
   clay;
And Jackson's in the bushes, trying to get
   away.

Jim had used Sam's money and didn't
   want to pay;
He thought his only chance was to give
   poor Sam away.

He sold out Sam and Barnes and left their
   friends to mourn—
Oh, what a scorching Jim will get when
   Gabriel blows his horn!

And so he sold out Sam and Barnes and
   left their friends to mourn.
Oh, what a scorching Jim will get when
   Gabriel blows his horn!

Perhaps he's got to heaven, there's none of
   us can say;
But if I'm right in my surmise, he's gone
   the other way.

What Bass didn't know was that Murphy had made a deal with Major John B. Jones, a Texas Ranger. In exchange for dropping charges against his family—and a handsome reward—Murphy agreed to report on Bass's whereabouts.

Some of the other members of the Bass gang were suspicious of Murphy, but he managed to get word to Jones that the outlaws were planning to hit the Round Rock bank. On the afternoon of July 15, 1878, Bass and three others rode into Round Rock. A group of Texas Rangers were there waiting for them. As Jim Murphy watched from his hiding spot, the outlaws shot it out with two of the town's deputy sheriffs and a gang of rangers. Shot in the stomach, Bass fled on horseback. But Murphy had seen that Bass was seriously wounded, and set the rangers on the outlaw's trail.

The rangers soon found Bass, whose right hand had also been hit by a bullet. Two of his fingers had been shot off. But that was the least of Bass's troubles. He had lost a great deal of blood from his stomach wound. A doctor who arrived with the posse said that he wouldn't survive. The doctor was right. Bass died two days later—on his twenty-seventh birthday—having refused to inform on the other gang members. Asked who had planned the raid with him, Bass reportedly said "It's agin [against] my trade to blow [tell] on my pals. If a man knows anything, he ought to die with it in him."

Jim Murphy, the gang member who turned against Sam Bass, died under strange circumstances one year after the outlaw's death. He swallowed atrophine, an eye medication. Some said it was an accident, while others claimed it was suicide.

Sources for Further Reading

The American West, A Cultural Encyclopedia, Volume 1. Danbury, CT: Grolier Educational Corp., 1995, pp. 80–81.

Nash, Jay Robert. *Bloodletters and Badmen.* New York: M. Evans, 1973, pp. 46–49.

Prassel, Frank Richard. *The Great American Outlaw, A Legacy of Fact and Fiction.* Norman, OK: University of Oklahoma Press, 1993, pp. 139–142, 338–340.

Ross, Stewart. *Fact or Fiction: Bandits & Outlaws.* Surrey, British Columbia: Copper Beech Books, 1995, p. 37.

Billy the Kid
(William Bonney)

Born: September 17, 1859
Died: July 14, 1881
AKA: Henry Antrim,
Kid Antrim, Henry McCarty

One of the most famous outlaws of the Old West, Billy the Kid never robbed a bank or a stagecoach and probably killed no more than a half-dozen men. However, when the man responsible for killing the Kid wrote a sensationalized book about him, fact and fiction became forever blurred.

A SKETCHY PAST

Everyone has heard of Billy the Kid—but no one knows who he really was. It's generally accepted that he was born in the slums of New York City, although other sources place his birth in Indiana. (One version of Billy's life claims that he was born in Ireland to a peasant father and Native American mother.) William Bonney was probably an alias (assumed name), that he took later in life. Some authorities believe that his real name was Henry McCarty—the son of Patrick Henry McCarty and Catherine Devine McCarty. The couple also had an older son, Joseph.

Billy's father died sometime in the 1860s—possibly while fighting in the Civil War (1861–1865). Billy's widowed mother moved West, and eventually married a man named William Antrim. Antrim moved the family to the boom town of Silver Springs, New Mexico, where he worked as a miner. With no school to attend, Billy, who was still just a boy, received little education.

Billy's mother died when he was fifteen years old, and his reputation as a killer seems to have developed shortly there-

There's no shortage of movies about the infamous Billy the Kid. *The Left-Handed Gun* and *Pat Garrett and Billy the Kid* are among the best. An offbeat account of the Kid's exploits, *The Left-Handed Gun* (1958) portrays Billy as a young rebel without a cause. (In fact the title role, played by Paul Newman, was originally intended for James Dean, the star of *Rebel Without a Cause,* the story of a troubled teenager.)

Widely considered to be a masterpiece, *Pat Garrett and Billy the Kid* (1973) tells the Kid's story in flashback, as he spends his final days at Fort Sumner. Garrett (played by James Coburn) is portrayed as a lawman who has no choice but to kill his former friend, Billy (played by Kris Kristofferson).

Identification, Please.

Many sources list Billy's birthdate as November 23. Some authorities believe that the date was made up by Ash Upson, one of Billy the Kid's first biographers—whose own birthday fell on the same date!

after. Some sources claim young Billy left Arizona to flee from a petty theft charge. Others claim he murdered a man with a pen knife. Whatever really happened, Billy left Silver Springs. In Arizona, in 1877—when Billy was just seventeen years old—he shot and killed a blacksmith named "Windy" Cahill in a saloon fight. It was the Kid's first documented killing. The *Arizona Citizen* published the coroner's verdict concerning the killing. The coroner concluded that the killing was "criminal and unjustifiable, and that Henry Antrim, alias Kid, was guilty thereof." The legend of the Kid was off and running.

CATTLE WARS AND KILLINGS

The Kid soon resurfaced in Lincoln County, in southeastern New Mexico. At the time, Lincoln County covered a great deal of territory (several times more than it does today). It was the land of cattle barons, where rival factions were waging war with one another. The violence came to a head in 1878 in what has come to be known as the Lincoln County War.

Billy worked on the ranch of John Tunstall, an educated Englishman. A number of other wealthy cattle owners were native to the area, and resented Tunstall as a newcomer who threatened their livelihood. Lawrence Murphy and James Dolan were among the men who opposed Tunstall. The Englishman withstood threats and harassment. But on February 18, 1878, he was killed.

The Kid seems to have been very fond of Tunstall. Some sources claim that Billy adopted the Englishman as a father-figure. But in truth, the two didn't know each other for long before Tunstall was killed. Whatever his motivation, Billy joined forces with Tunstall's men to seek revenge for his murder. The group, known as the "Regulators," tracked and killed many of Murphy and Dolan's associates. On April 1, 1878, Billy took part in the ambush killing of Sheriff William Brady, who had set in motion the plot against Tunstall.

The killing of Brady—who was also a deputy U.S. marshal—did not go unnoticed. A huge posse (a group of people with legal authority to capture criminals) and a troop of cavalrymen tracked Billy and his companions. When the lawmen found the Regulators hiding in the home of one of Tunstall's associates, a tremendous gun battle followed. After days of shooting, some members of the posse set the house on fire. When Billy and the others fled the burning building, some were killed—but Billy managed to escape.

NO PARDON FOR THE KID

Billy somehow arranged to make a deal to be pardoned by Governor Lew Wallace, who had been appointed by President Rutherford B. Hayes with specific instructions to bring law and order to Lincoln County. According to some sources, Billy was to receive a full pardon in exchange for testifying against three men who had killed a lawyer. Billy still had to stand trial for the sheriff's murder, but the governor promised he would go free—no matter what the verdict was.

The governor was surprised at Billy's popularity with the people of Lincoln County. In a letter to a friend, he wrote, "A precious specimen nicknamed 'The Kid' whom the Sheriff is holding here in the Plaza, as it is called, is an object of tender regard. I heard singing and music the other night; going to the door, I found the minstrels [musicians] of the village actually serenading the fellow in his prison." Billy testified against the lawyer's killers, but he didn't wait to find out if the governor was a man of his word. Billy left town before his own trial began.

By now, Billy needed money. He asked John Chisum—a cattle baron he had worked for—to pay him back wages. When Chisum refused, Billy organized a gang of outlaws to steal his livestock. For a year and a half, from the summer of 1879 to the end of 1880, Billy headed a band of horse and cattle thieves. Governor Wallace, who was angry that Billy had run away from

Captured: A Boy with Winning Ways

Billy's capture was big news. Newspapers around the country reported the details of his last stand (although many false accounts of his capture had already been published). The incident was front-page news in Las Vegas papers—one of which printed:

> He looked and acted a mere boy. He is about five feet eight or nine inches tall, slightly built and lithe [graceful], weighing about 140; a frank open countenance [expression], looking like a school boy, with the traditional silky fuzz on his upper lip; clear blue eyes, with a roguish snap about them; light hair and complexion. He is, in all, quite a handsome looking fellow, the only imperfection being two prominent front teeth slightly protruding like squirrel's teeth, and he has agreeable and winning ways.

his trial, posted a $500 reward for the capture of the Kid.

SURRENDER AT STINKING SPRINGS

In November of 1880, a new player entered the picture. Patrick Floyd Garrett, a former acquaintance of Billy's, was elected as sheriff of Lincoln County. An expert gunman, Garrett knew the area well and was supported by the cattle ranchers. And he was determined to rid the county of the notorious Billy the Kid. Because he had known Billy, some people in the county regarded Garrett as a traitor, who had turned against a friend.

For a while, Billy's informants managed to help him avoid capture. But in December, Garrett learned that the outlaws would be riding near Fort Sumner. A former army post, Fort Sumner was used as a ranch by a friend of Billy's. On December 18, Garrett organized a number of detectives and ambushed Billy and members of his gang at Fort Sumner. One of the outlaws—the Kid's friend, Tom O'Folliard—was killed in the gunfire, while Billy and the others escaped.

The Garrett posse had little trouble tracking the outlaws in the snow. Their trail led to a deserted cabin east of Sumner, at Stinking Springs. There, the sheriff's men surrounded the cabin, demanding that the outlaws surrender. Refusing, the outlaws fired their guns at the posse. Rather than risk the lives of his men, Garrett decided to try a different approach. The posse waited until the outlaws had run out of food. Within a few days, Billy and his associates surrendered.

JAIL BREAK!

After he was taken to Mesilla, New Mexico, Billy was tried for murder. Since he had broken the terms of his agreement with Governor Wallace, he no longer had any hope of a pardon.

Convicted of murder by a jury, Billy was sentenced to hang in Lincoln on May 13, 1881. As the story goes, the judge sentenced Billy to hang "until you are dead, dead, dead," to which the outlaw responded, "And you can go to hell, hell, hell."

A couple of Garrett's men took Billy back to Lincoln, where he was kept under guard on the top floor of the court house. He sent many letters to Governor Wallace demanding a pardon—but his pleas fell on deaf ears. On April 28, 1881—just a couple of weeks before his execution was to take place—Billy escaped from jail. No one is sure exactly how the jail break occurred. But *somehow,* Billy managed to get hold of a pistol. (Some say a girl who was in love with the outlaw hid the gun in an outhouse, while other sources claim he managed to wrestle the pistol away from one of the guards after his handcuffs had been loosened at mealtime.) In any case, Billy shot and killed James Bell, one of the guards, and then killed Deputy Bob Ollinger when he ran into the room to see what had happened. Sheriff Pat Garrett was out of town at the time.

Pat Garrett, the man who took out Billy the Kid.

Billy escaped with a couple of guns and a Winchester rifle. After he forced a blacksmith to remove the shackles on his hands and feet, he stole a horse and roared out of town. Hiding in familiar territory, Billy remained in the area of Fort Sumner—something that has puzzled historians since the day he died. Why didn't he flee to an area—such as Old Mexico—where he wasn't well known? Some say a girlfriend kept him from leaving, but he was known as a man who always looked out for himself above anyone else. Others think that hopes of revenge might have kept him from vanishing from the territory.

THE END OF THE LINE

Whatever his reasons, Billy didn't leave the area. On July 14, 1881, Garrett went to the home of Pete Maxwell, a sheep rancher who lived near Fort Sumner—perhaps in response to a tip that the outlaw was hiding there. What happened next varies

Pat Garrett: The Man Who Shot Billy the Kid

Patrick Floyd Jarvis Garrett was born in Alabama in 1850. Raised in Louisiana, he moved to Texas when he was in his twenties in order to work as a cattle herder and buffalo hunter. By 1878, hunting was no longer a productive occupation since much of the buffalo population in Texas had been killed off. Garrett—an expert shot and skilled horseman—moved West to New Mexico, where cattle owners were battling rustlers who were stealing their stock.

Garrett tried a number of activities, including ranching and tending bar. Eventually, the citizens of Lincoln County, New Mexico, asked the six-foot-five-inch former buffalo hunter to be the sheriff. Immediately after he was appointed to the office, Sheriff Garrett made clear his intention to bring in the notorious Billy the Kid. With the help of detectives from the cattle lands in Texas, Garrett relentlessly tracked the Kid and killed him.

Some people praised Garrett as a hero for killing the Kid, while others criticized him for failing to give the outlaw a fair chance in a fight. The sheriff later described how he felt the evening he from one story to another, but the ending is always the same: Garrett shot and killed Billy the Kid. According to some sources, Garrett killed the Kid in cold blood—possibly in his sleep. According to the sheriff himself, he bravely faced the fugitive outlaw in a darkened room at the Maxwell home. In Garrett's own words, this is how it happened:

> Maxwell whispered to me. "That's him!" Simultaneously [at the same time] the Kid must have seen, or felt, the presence of a third person at the head of the bed. He raised quickly his pistol, a self-cocker, within a foot of my breast. Retreating rapidly across the room he cried: *"Quien es? Quien es?"* ["Who's that? Who's that?"] All this occurred in a moment. Quickly as possible I drew my revolver and fired, threw my body aside, and fired again. The second shot was useless; the Kid fell dead.

> —**The Authentic Life of Billy the Kid** *(1882), by Pat Garrett*

Billy was dead at the age of twenty-one. Although legend claimed that he had killed a man for every year of his life, the actual figure was probably between six and nine. A local judge immediately ruled that Garrett had shot Billy in the line of duty.

Billy's grave
Today, the exact location of Billy's grave is unknown-- the original wood marker has disappeared. According to legend, no flowers will grow there.

killed the Kid: "Scared? . . . Wouldn't you have been scared? . . . Well, I should say so. I started out on that expedition with the expectation of getting scared. I went out contemplating the probability of being . . . killed; but not if any precaution [a measure to prevent harm] on my part would prevent such a catastrophe [disaster]."

With the help of writer Ash Upson, Garrett wrote *The Authentic Life of Billy the Kid,* published one year after the outlaw's death. The purpose of the book was not to document history—but to make money. Filled with fictional and exaggerated accounts of Billy's exploits, it is the source of many of the inaccuracies in the legend of Billy the Kid. (Many of Billy's later biographers relied on *The Authentic Life* for the "facts" of the outlaw's life.) In spite of everything, the book was a financial failure.

Garrett's career after the killing of Billy the Kid was anything but noteworthy. He tried his hand at farming and ranching, and also served a two-year term as a customs collector in El Paso, Texas. On February 29, 1908, he was shot to death. Historians still argue about who his killer was. No one was ever convicted of the crime.

The outlaw was buried in a military cemetery at Fort Sumner. At his grave was a marker that bore the words, *"Duerme bien, Querido,"* meaning "Sleep well, beloved."

Sources for Further Reading

The American West, A Cultural Encyclopedia, Volumes 1 and 4. Danbury, CT: Grolier Educational Corp., 1995, pp. 102–105, 612–613.

Nash, Jay Robert. *Bloodletters and Badmen.* New York: M. Evans, 1973, pp. 66–71.

Prassel, Frank Richard. *The Great American Outlaw, A Legacy of Fact and Fiction.* Norman, OK: University of Oklahoma Press, 1993, pp. 144–161, 327–330, 340.

Rosa, Joseph. *The Taming of the West: Age of the Gunfighter.* New York: Smithmark, 1993, pp. 76–83.

Shenkman, Richard and Kurt Reiger. *One Night Stands with American History.* New York: Quill, 1982, p. 197.

Vandome, Nick. *Crimes and Criminals.* New York: Chambers, 1992, pp. 30–31.

Wukovits, John. *The Gunslingers.* Broomall, PA: Chelsea House, 1997, pp. 25–32.

The Buck Gang

Active: July 28-August 10, 1895

In July of 1895, a small gang led by Rufus Buck embarked on a thirteen-day crime spree. For reasons that have never been explained, the group of five young, uneducated men committed a series of robberies, rapes, and murders in the Indian Territory to the west of Arkansas.

THIRTEEN DAYS OF DEVASTATION

The gang's rampage began on July 28 when they met in Okmulgee, Oklahoma, to arm themselves with guns and rifles. John Garrett, an African American U.S. deputy marshal, approached the young men to ask why they were heavily armed. Rufus and the others opened fire on the deputy, killing him.

Traveling between Muskogee and Fort Smith, Arkansas, the young men robbed a number of shopkeepers and ranch owners. Later they raped at least two women—a widow named Wilson and Rosetta Hassan, a farmer's wife. Next they robbed a drummer named Callahan, killing a boy who worked for him by shooting him in the back. The young men showed no sympathy for their victims: they threatened to harm infants and reportedly made some of their victims "dance" by shooting at their feet.

THEY HANGED THEM HIGH

News of the Buck gang's activities soon reached the territory's lawmen and a large posse (a group of people with legal

The Buck Gang, with Rufus Buck in the center, await their trial in 1895.

authority to capture criminals) of federal marshals was sent to capture the outlaws. With them went a company of Creek Indian police—or Creek Lighthorsemen. Trapped near Muskogee, the gang attempted to shoot their way past the posse, but they were outnumbered. On August 10, 1895, all five gang members were captured and taken into custody.

The five men were taken to the town of McDermott, Oklahoma—near the site of two of the gang's robberies—where angry citizens threatened to lynch them. (Lynchings, usually performed by mobs, are illegal killings. Most often, the victims are hanged.) Chained to one another to prevent escape, they were secretly taken out of town to Fort Smith, Arkansas, a town they had previously terrorized. Although the Creeks wanted to try the gang members under tribal law, the young men went to

Judge Isaac Parker's court of the damned

Rufus Buck and the four other members of his gang weren't the only criminals to be sentenced to death by Judge Isaac Charles Parker. During his twenty-one years on the bench, Parker sentenced over one hundred seventy-two men to death—of whom eighty-eight were killed. (The numbers would have been higher if it weren't for presidential pardons and other acts.) Known as the "hanging judge," Parker sentenced more men to death than any other judge of his time. When pronouncing a death sentence, Parker reportedly said, "I do not desire to hang you men. It is the law." (He was also said to cry when he delivered the sentence.)

Although hanging was not the only sentence prescribed for murder, Parker always condemned convicted murderers—for which his court became known as the Court of the Damned. Concerning the sentencing of murderers, Parker stated, "This court is but the humble instrument to aid in the execution of that divine justice which has ever decided that he who takes what he cannot return—the life of another human being—shall lose his own."

Parker studied law on his own and was admitted to the Missouri bar in 1859. Following brief service in the Civil War (1861–1865), he became an attorney in St. Joseph, Missouri, in 1862. After serving four years as Missouri's republican congressman, Parker was appointed as a federal judge by President Ulysses S. Grant in 1875. (Parker had already turned down an offer to assume the position of chief justice of the Utah Territory.) Parker's jurisdiction, or territory—the Western District of Arkansas—included the Indian Territory (now Oklahoma), an area ravaged by crime. In his first eight-week session, Parker tried eighteen defendants for murder; of the fifteen who were convicted, six were sentenced to death. A man who stood six feet tall, weighing two hundred pounds, Parker reportedly held court six days a week, from 8:30 in the morning until after dark.

Parker appointed two hundred deputy marshals—many of them African Americans and

trial before Judge Isaac Parker, who was known as the "hanging judge." A number of their victims testified, including Rosetta Hassan and her husband. At the end of the brief trial, one of the defense lawyers reportedly concluded his argument saying, "May it please the court and the gentlemen of the jury, you have heard the evidence. I have nothing to say."

Each of the gang members was convicted of rape. The jury reportedly handed down its verdict without even sitting in the

Native Americans. Bass Reeves, an African American who served as federal marshal for thirty-five years, was one of Parker's most effective deputies. Charged with policing a rough territory, "the men who rode for Parker" were paid by a fee system. For bringing in prisoners, marshals earned ten cents a mile, one way. The "guardsmen" earned two dollars a day. Many of these men paid a high price for their work. Over the twenty-one years Parker was in office, at least sixty-five of his marshals were killed in the line of duty.

Parker's court also had a record-setting conviction rate. The judge issued 8,600 convictions and 1,700 acquittals—which means *5 out of 6* prisoners tried in Parker's court were found guilty. Although judges are expected to be impartial, Parker was in the habit of "leading" the jury, or letting the jurors know what he thought about a case. He once said: "I have been accused of leading juries. I tell you a jury should be led! If they are guided they will render justice." Parker also had his own ideas about evidence—which forced members of the Supreme Court to remind him that the government's rules of evidence applied to

his court as much as any other. Objections such as these prompted Parker to complain about the Supreme Court's "laxity" (lack of authority) and concern for the "flimsiest technicalities."

Up until 1889, the Supreme Court did not allow prisoners who were convicted in Parker's court to appeal the judge's decision. That year, forty-six cases were reconsidered by the Supreme Court. The High Court decided that *thirty* of the men Parker had condemned to die had received an unfair trial. In 1895, Congress removed the Indian Territory from Parker's jurisdiction. He died the following year—the year the Buck gang was executed—before the formal transfer of the territory took place.

During his lifetime many people across the country had disapproved of Parker's justice—which often attracted large crowds to multiple public hangings. But after his death, many praised Parker—who had championed Women's Suffrage (the women's rights movement) and had supported the rights of Native Americans—as one of the greatest judges in the American West.

jury room. After the verdict was announced, Judge Parker informed the gang members that he considered the crime they were convicted of to be equal to murder. He said:

> I want to say in this case that the jury, under the law and the evidence, could come to no other conclusion than that which they arrived at. Their verdict is an entirely just one, and one that must be approved by all lovers of virtue. The offense of which you have

been convicted is one that shocks all men who are not brutal. It is known to the law as a crime offensive to decency, and as a brutal attack upon the honor and chastity of the weaker sex . . . it has been by the lawmakers of the United States deemed equal in enormity and wickedness to murder, because the punishment fixed by the same is that which follows the commission of the crime of murder.

Parker sentenced the five young men to hang on October 31, 1895. But sometime after the trial, Rufus Buck claimed that he was not involved in the crimes and could provide an alibi—proof that he was elsewhere when the rapes were committed. Parker delayed the execution while the gang's lawyers appealed the verdict. (In an appeal, a case is taken to a higher court to be reheard.) After the U.S. Supreme Court declined to hear the case, Parker set a new date for the mass hanging: July 1, 1896. The execution was not postponed. Almost one year after they were captured, the five gang members were hanged—together, on one large scaffold—at Fort Smith. While three of the gang members were said to have died instantly, of broken necks, Rufus Buck and Lucky Davis struggled on the gallows as they slowly strangled to death.

Following the execution, a prison guard found a poem that Rufus Buck had written on the backside of a photograph of his mother. The poem, titled "My Dream," was full of odd spellings, punctuation, and misplaced capitals. Here is Rufus Buck's poem:

> MY, dream. —1896
> i, dremp'T, i, was, in heAven,
> Among, The, AngeLs, Fair;
> i'd, neAr, seen, none, so HAndsome,
> THAT, Twine, in golden HAir,
> They, looked, so, neAT, and; sAng, so, sweeT,
> And, PLAY'd, The, The, goLden, HArp,
> i, wAs, About, To, Pick An, ANgeL, ouT,
> And, Take, Her, To, mY, HeArT,
> BuT, The, momenT, i, BegAn, To, PLeA,
> i, THougHT, oF, You, mY, Love,
> There, wAs, none i'd, seen, so BeAuTiFuLL,
> On, eArTH, or HeAven, ABove,
> gooD, By, My. Dear. Wife, AnD. MoTHer
> all. so, My, sisTer

RUFUS BUCK
youse. Truley
1 Day. of. JUly
Tu, The, Yeore
off 1896

TRANSLATION:

I dreamt I was in Heaven
Among the Angels fair;
I'd never seen any so handsome,
That are entwined in golden hair.
They looked so neat and sang so sweet
And played the golden harp.
I was about to pick an angel out
And take her to my heart.
But the moment I began to plea,
I thought of you, my love.
There was none I'd ever seen so beautiful
On earth or Heaven above,
Goodbye my dear wife and Mother.
Also my sister.
Rufus Buck,
Yours truly.
July 1, Tuesday, 1896

Sources for Further Reading

The American West, A Cultural Encyclopedia, Volume 7. Danbury, CT: Grolier Educational Corp., 1995, pp. 1193–1194.

Cusic, Don. *Cowboys and the Wild West, An A to Z Guide from the Chisholm Trail to the Silver Screen.* New York: Facts on File, 1994, p. 220.

Nash, Jay Robert. *Bloodletters and Badmen.* New York: M. Evans, 1973, p. 90

Nash, Jay Robert. *Encyclopedia of World Crime.* Wilmette, IL: Crime Books, 1990, pp. 531–532.

Rosa, Joseph G. *The Taming of the West: Age of the Gunfighter.* New York: Smithmark, 1993, pp. 136–137.

Sifakis, Carl. *The Encyclopedia of American Crime.* New York: Facts on File, 1982, p. 105.

Calamity Jane
(Martha Jane Cannary)

Born: May 1, 1852?
Died: August 1, 1903
AKA: M. E. Burke

Calamity Jane—although not exactly an outlaw—was unconventional. At a time when women did not wear men's clothing, go to bars, or appear in public drunk, she did so— and then some. A hard-bitten alcoholic, she died in her early fifties, aged far beyond her years.

AN UNCONVENTIONAL CHILDHOOD

Like many other frontier figures, Calamity Jane was a legend in her own time. Tall tales about her exploits traveled from town to town throughout the West. Dime novels published in the East printed episodes from her life—most of which had little to do with the truth. And Calamity Jane's autobiography (a biography written by the subject) was no more reliable. Printed and distributed when Calamity Jane was a theatrical attraction, the "autobiography" presented a sensational—and often fictional—account of her life.

Even the simplest details about Calamity Jane's life are uncertain. She might have been born in Illinois, Missouri, or Wyoming. Her father could have been a minister, an army man, or a gambler. According to one version, she was born near Fort Laramie, Wyoming, and orphaned at an early age when Indians killed and scalped her parents.

In spite of the many stories, it is generally accepted that Calamity Jane was born on May 1, 1852, near Princeton, Missouri, to a farmer named Robert Cannary (or Canary) and his wife, Charlotte. The original Cannary farm was purchased by Cannary's grandfather in 1855. Four years later, Robert Cannary added 108 acres to the family's plot—at a cost of $500. He worked the farm with his father until the older man died in 1859. Thornton Cannary, Robert's brother, lived on the opposite side of Mercer County and established himself as one of the state's largest landowners. The oldest of five children, Martha Jane—who was later known as "Calamity Jane"—soon earned a reputation as a wild and high-spirited child.

What's in a name?

Calamity Jane probably received her nickname sometime in the early 1870s. Historians disagree as to how she came to be known as "Calamity." Cannary reportedly claimed that she had gotten the name from Army captain Pat Egan, whom she had saved from an Indian attack. "Jane," he supposedly said, "you're a wonderful little woman to have around in time of calamity. From now on your name's Calamity Jane." The story is now part of the Calamity Jane myth—but Cannary made it up.

Some historians speculate that the name "Calamity" came about as a reference to what would happen to those who did not take sharpshooter's guns seriously. Others still consider it to be a reference to Jane's calamitous, hard-luck life.

According to Calamity Jane's autobiography—if portions of it can be believed—Martha Jane Cannary traveled with her family on the Overland Route to the gold-rush town of Virginia City, Montana, in 1865. During the five-month journey that covered approximately two thousand miles, Cannary learned to drive teams of oxen. She became an expert at using a bullwhacker—a thirty-foot whip that teamsters used to drive animals. According to her autobiography, she spent much of her time with men. She wrote that she was "at all times with the men when there was excitement and adventures to be had."

By the age of fifteen, Cannary was orphaned—after both parents died within a year of one another. Little is known of her activities until the early 1870s, when she surfaced in Rawlins, Wyoming. Tall and solidly built, she dressed in men's clothing and worked at jobs that were not usually available to women—such as railroad work, which entailed swinging a heavy pick and laying railroad ties; bullwhacking, or driving teams of bulls carrying supplies to mining camps; and mule skinning, or driving mules from one point to another.

Calamity's daughter

In June 1941, a woman who called herself Mrs. Jane Hickok McCormick, a native of Billings, Montana, claimed that she was the daughter of Calamity Jane and Wild Bill Hickok. To prove her identity, she produced a diary and confession that were supposedly written by her mother. The diary consists of a series of letters that are sometimes years apart. The first letter, addressed to her daughter, is dated September 25, 1877. It reads in part:

My Dear:

This isn't intended for a diary and it may even happen that this may never be sent to you. But I would like to think of you reading it someday, page by page, in the years to come after my death. I would like to hear you laugh when you look at these pictures of meself. I am alone in the shack and tired. I rode sixty miles yesterday to the post office and returned today. This is your birthday. You are four years old today. Jim [James O'Neil, the man who reportedly adopted Cannary's daughter] promised me he would always get a letter to me on your birthday each year. Was I glad to hear from him. He sent a tiny picture of you. You are the dead spit of meself at the same age. . . .

The diary and confession have never been authenticated. And Mrs. McCormick's relationship to Calamity Jane and Hickok has never been proven.

A GIRL SCOUT

Cannary wrote in her autobiography that she spent the years between 1868 and 1876 serving as an Army scout on various expeditions. She claimed to have worked with General George Armstrong Custer and other renowned Army officials—but Army records fail to mention her service. The many errors in Cannary's accounts of her scouting expeditions have caused historians to doubt their truth. There is no real evidence that she ever worked as an Army scout.

But Cannary did accompany Army expeditions—possibly as a bullwhacker or simply as a hanger-on. According to some sources, she traveled with General George Crook's expedition against the Sioux Indians in 1875—and was forced to return home when her gender was found out as she swam in the nude. Cannary herself claimed to have delivered messages from General Crook to General Custer by swimming across the Platte

River. Another story has her following a young soldier she met while working in a brothel. Dressed as a man, she followed the soldier's detachment into the Black Hills of Dakota. It seems likely that she did venture into the Black Hills with Crook's soldiers in 1876: one of Crook's men reported that "Calamity Jane is hear [here] going up with the troops." Cannary spent the next four years in the Black Hills—at a time when gold fever was at its peak.

WILD BILL

Historians generally agree that Cannary was associated with Wild Bill Hickok in Deadwood, Dakota Territory, in 1876. But they don't all agree on the nature of their relationship. Cannary claimed in her autobiography to have been married to Hickok. Despite evidence to the contrary, the legend that the couple was secretly married continues to thrive. Some biographers claim that she was little more than a bar-room acquaintance of the famous shootist known as "the Prince of the Pistoleers." Still others argue that there is no evidence that the two ever met.

Hickok, who claimed to be devoted to his wife, Agnes, was shot and killed by a man named Jack McCall on August 2, 1876. Cannary later boasted that she had helped to hang McCall. In truth, however, McCall was legally hanged after a court at Yankton, South Dakota, found him guilty of murder.

CALAMITY JANE, MEDICINE WOMAN

Cannary had a reputation as a hard-drinking, rowdy, foul-mouthed ruffian. But she was also known as a generous, kind-hearted woman who was never mean-spirited, even when drunk. When a smallpox epidemic struck Deadwood in 1878, she stepped forward to help take care of the sick miners by providing them with food, drink, and clean clothing.

The testimony of her contemporaries prevents this incident from being written off as part of the legend of Calamity Jane: a man named Babcock, the town's only doctor, later confirmed that Cannary volunteered to help the smallpox-stricken people

A young girl stands over the grave of Calamity Jane in Deadwood, South Dakota.

who were housed in a shack on the outskirts of town. A number of Deadwood natives were later quoted as saying that they owed their lives to Cannary.

MRS. BURKE

Cannary left Deadwood in 1880. For the next fifteen years, she traveled around the Dakotas, Kansas, Montana, and Wyoming. In August 1885, according to her autobiography, she married a hack driver (horse-drawn carriage driver) from Texas named Clinton Burke—although there is no legal evidence of any such marriage. (She apparently had a habit of referring to any man she lived with as her husband.) Later in life, Cannary called herself Mrs. M. E. Burke—a name that is inscribed, beneath "Calamity Jane" on her tombstone.

Cannary also claimed to have had a child—a daughter, who was born on October 28, 1887—although many people believed that the girl was in fact Burke's child by another woman. According to popular theory, the child was raised by Burke's relatives. Before long, Burke disappeared from Cannary's life.

Take a look at this!

The Paleface (1948), starring Bob Hope and Jane Russell, is the story of a cowardly dentist who becomes a gunslinging hero when Calamity Jane starts aiming for him. A nutty comedy, it turns conventions of the Old West upside down. And if you like that, check out the sequel—*The Son of Paleface* (1952).

ALL THE WORLD'S A STAGE

Cannary continued to drift from one town to another. She worked at various jobs to support herself—and sometimes turned to prostitution. Her drinking binges sometimes lasted for days, and her physical condition began to deteriorate. In 1896 she worked for an amusement company in Minneapolis, Minnesota, appearing on stage dressed as an Army scout—in a buckskin outfit and moccasins, carrying six-shooters and a Winchester rifle. In order to stir up public interest, she sold copies of her seven-page autobiography, in which she spun sensational tales about her exploits as a scout.

Suffering from alcoholism, Cannary missed many performances and was eventually fired from her job. In May 1900, a newspaper editor and novelist reportedly found her living in a brothel. They convinced her to travel east to Buffalo, New York, where she took a job performing in a western show at the Pan-American Exposition. She did not stay long. According to legend, "Buffalo Bill" Cody, a western showman, sent her back to the West after Cannary complained that she was homesick for her native land. Whether Cody was responsible or not, Cannary returned to the West, where she continued to drift and drink.

In July 1903, she arrived at the Calloway Hotel in Terry, near Deadwood, in Dakota Territory. Ravaged by alcoholism and impoverished, she died in early August of "inflammation of the bowels." Local women dressed her body in a clean dress and an undertaker donated a pine coffin. On August 4, Cannary was buried at Mt. Moriah Cemetery—in one of the largest funerals the residents of Deadwood had ever seen. She was buried next to Wild Bill Hickok.

Sources for Further Reading

Horan, James. *Desperate Women*. New York: Putnam, 1952, pp. 171–200.

James, Edward T., ed. *Notable American Women,* Volume 1. Cambridge, MA: Belknap Press, 1971, pp. 267–268.

Johnson, Thomas H., ed. *The Oxford Companion to American History*. New York: Oxford University Press, 1966, p. 129.

Lamar, Howard Roberts. *The Reader's Encyclopedia of the American West*. New York: Harper & Row, 1977, pp. 146–147.

The McGraw-Hill Encyclopedia of World Biography. New York: McGraw-Hill Book Company, 1973, pp. 320–321.

Butch Cassidy
(Robert Leroy Parker)

Born: April 6, 1866
Died: ?
AKA: George Cassidy, Jim Ryan

A likable and intelligent young man, Butch Cassidy participated in a number of successful bank and train robberies in the American West at the end of the nineteenth century. He was a member of a group of outlaws known as the Wild Bunch—most of whom were either killed or imprisoned.

A MORMON CATTLE THIEF

Robert Leroy Parker was born in 1866 in the Sevier River country near Circleville, Utah. Ten years before he was born, his father and grandparents had crossed the Great Plains as "hand-cart pioneers." They carried their possessions across the plains by walking and pulling carts behind them. One of ten children, Robert was raised on a small ranch. Like many of the people who settled in Utah, his parents were Mormons—a group of Christians that follows strict moral guidelines. (Although Parker's father, Maximillian Parker, was said to have had a rebellious streak.)

Growing up, Parker received no formal education. Instead, he was "educated" in the art of cattle rustling by Mike Cassidy, a cowboy-rustler who worked for his father. Under Cassidy's supervision, Parker learned how to rope and brand animals, and he became an expert rider and marksman. In short, he learned all the skills required to become a horse and cattle thief. While still a teenager, Parker accompanied Cassidy on long cattle drives in the neighboring mountain ranges.

The Wild Bunch: (standing, left to right) William Carver, Harvey Logan; (sitting, left to right) the Sundance Kid (Harry Longbaugh), Ben Kilpatrick, and Butch Cassidy.

Frequently in trouble with the law, Cassidy headed south after the shooting of a Wyoming rancher. Parker—who had been Cassidy's right-hand man—took over his cattle-rustling business. And he took his last name, too. (In Parker's day, it was common for an outlaw to adopt the name of another criminal whose crimes and misdeeds he admired.) Robert Leroy Parker went by the name of George Cassidy. Later—after brief work as a butcher—he became known as Butch Cassidy.

EN ROUTE TO THE ROBBERS' ROOST

Butch Cassidy soon left Utah and took an honest job in Telluride, in southwest Colorado. For a while, he packed ore by muleback from the mines to the mill. But it wasn't long before

The Sundance Kid

After his release from the Wyoming penitentiary, Butch Cassidy helped to rob a bank in Montpelier, Idaho, and fled to the Robber's Roost. The Robber's Roost was an isolated hideout in southeastern Utah. There, he met Harry Longabaugh—better known as the Sundance Kid. The two soon struck up a lifelong friendship.

Not much is known about Longabaugh's background. He was probably born in Pennsylvania in 1863, and eventually headed West. As a young man, he served an extended sentence for horse theft. Imprisoned in Sundance, Wyoming, Longabaugh later became known as the Sundance Kid.

Longabaugh became a member of the Wild Bunch—also known as the Hole-in-the-Wall Gang, named after one of the gang's favorite hideaways. An expert gunslinger, he had lightning reflexes, and was known as one of the fastest and most accurate shooters in the West. Unlike many of his counterparts, he is said to have worn only one gun. In spite of his deadly aim, Longabaugh was said to be a quiet man who was slow to draw his weapon.

After the Wild Bunch broke up, Longabaugh escaped with Butch Cassidy to South America, where they continued to rob banks and trains. What became of the two outlaws has become the subject of much debate. Some historians believe that Longabaugh and Cassidy died in a shoot-out with Bolivian soldiers. Others believe Longabaugh escaped. According to one story—made popular by a man who claimed to be the son of the Sundance Kid—Longabaugh fled to the United States, where he married his girlfriend, Etta Place, and lived happily ever after until 1957, when he died peacefully at the age of ninety-four.

he fell in with a group of bandits known as the McCarty gang—run by the McCarty brothers, Tom and Bill. They asked Cassidy, who was twenty at the time, to help them rob a train. Cassidy joined the gang as they stopped the Denver and Rio Grande Express on November 3, 1887. The robbery was a complete failure. When the guard refused to open the safe, the outlaws were forced to ride away empty-handed.

The gang's next jobs were more successful. On March 30, 1889, they struck the First National Bank of Denver. Before a single shot was fired, the outlaws made off with $20,000 in bank notes. During this heist, Cassidy was said to have threatened to blow up the bank with a small bottle of nitroglycerin (liquid explosive). The bottle apparently contained nothing more than water. Cassidy and the other gang members headed for the Star Valley, a remote area on the Wyoming-Idaho border where bandits often hid.

Three months later—on June 24—the gang robbed a bank in Telluride. They struck at noontime and they struck fast. Without firing a shot, the outlaws left the bank with a sack filled with more than $10,000 in currency. Pursued by large posses (groups of people with legal authority to capture criminals), they escaped across rocky terrain by wrapping their horses' hooves in gunny sacks—a coarse fabric that allowed the horses to keep their footing on the slippery rock. The outlaws hid in canyons in an area called Robbers' Roost, along the lower Green River in southeastern Utah.

But more posses followed. Cassidy and the other gang members decided to lay low. For two years—from 1890 to 1892—Cassidy made an honest living, working as a cowboy in Colorado and Utah and as a butcher in Rock Springs, Wyoming.

TROUBLE WITH THE LAW

Eventually Cassidy tangled with the law. First, he was briefly jailed for disturbing the peace in a fight with a drunken man who had provoked him. After he was released, he went into business with Al Rainer, a cattle rustler. Together, they came up with a plan to make easy money. They rode from ranch to ranch in Colorado, promising the ranchers that they would protect their herds from cattle rustlers—for a fee. If the ranchers refused to pay the "protection" fee, Cassidy and Rainer resorted to "plan B." They stole the ranchers' cattle. Sometime in 1892 they were caught. That year, Cassidy's name appeared for the first time in court records.

Because of court delays, Cassidy's trial did not begin until July 4, 1894. Found guilty of cattle rustling, he was sentenced to two years in the Wyoming State Penitentiary. He was released early, thanks to a pardon issued by Governor William A. Richards. Cassidy is said to have made a deal with the governor in exchange for his pardon. According to some stories, he promised never to rustle cattle or rob another bank in Wyoming—although he said nothing about robbing trains or planning robberies for other outlaws in the state. Cassidy was released on January 19, 1896.

What's in a name?

Butch Cassidy and the Sundance Kid weren't the only outlaws in the Wild Bunch who went by assumed names. Many of the other gang members went by colorful nicknames—such as Deaf Charley (Camillo Hanks), the Tall Texan (Ben Kilpatrick), and Blackjack Ketchum (Thomas Ketchum). Often, they took a name that honored another outlaw. For example, Kid Curry (Harvey Logan) took his alias from an older bandit—Flat Nose George Curry (George Parrott).

A WILD BUNCH

Freed from jail, Cassidy headed straight for the Hole-in- the-Wall—an isolated hideout in the Colorado mountains where bandits and gunmen gathered. By the spring of 1896, Cassidy had joined up with a group of about twenty outlaws. "The Wild Bunch," as they were called, included ex-convicts Elza Lay and Bob Meeks, and Harvey Logan, a deadly man who was also known as Kid Curry. Sometime later, Harry Longabaugh—better known as the Sundance Kid—joined the Wild Bunch. Active in Wyoming, Colorado, and Utah, the Wild Bunch robbed about a dozen trains and banks over the next five years.

Many train robbers had failed because of stubborn guards or time-locked safes that prevented them from getting at their loot. But Cassidy and the Wild Bunch favored dynamite, which allowed them to get at the contents of locked safes by blowing them up. In one robbery, the gang used too much dynamite, and had to run up and down the railroad tracks to collect the bills that had been thrown from the train in the explosion.

Most of the Wild Bunch raids were very successful. (Although the Union Pacific train holdup at Tipton, Wyoming, brought the outlaws only fifty dollars.) The gang owed much of its success to intelligent planning—thanks largely to Butch Cassidy—and smooth execution, in which each robbery was carefully carried out according to plan. They studied the floor plans of banks and consulted timetables for trains they planned to rob. They bribed railroad workers to find out about shipments. They positioned fresh horses along the escape route so that they would be able to outrun the lawmen who pursued them. And they had carefully chosen hideouts along the "outlaw trail," where the gang members could come and go without being seen—and cross state borders to avoid capture.

THE END OF AN ERA

The Wild Bunch raided the Great Northern Flyer train near Wagner, Montana, on July 3, 1901. It would be the last heist they worked together. At Malta, Montana, Kid Curry boarded the train. When the Great Northern reached Wagner, he stepped into the engine room with a six-shooter (type of pistol) in each hand, and ordered the engineer to stop the locomotive. The Sundance Kid, who had been sitting in a coach car, kept passengers at bay by running up and down the aisles firing his guns. When the train came to a stop, Cassidy and other gang members boarded the train. Using dynamite to blow open the safe, the outlaws collected $40,000 in bank notes. But there was one problem: the notes weren't signed. In order to cash the notes, gang members had to forge the signature of the president of the bank.

By now the gang was being closely followed by lawmen and detectives from the Pinkerton Agency, who had been hired by the railroad companies. The detectives even had a photograph

of some of the outlaws. During a trip to Fort Worth, Texas, five members of the Wild Bunch had dressed in brand-new clothes to have their picture taken. As the story goes, Cassidy mailed a copy of the picture to the bank they had just robbed to thank them for their "contribution." The picture fell into the hands of Pinkerton detectives who were then able to identify the individual outlaws.

The Wild Bunch gang's days were numbered. New inventions like the telephone and the telegraph made it more and more difficult for the outlaws to escape from lawmen. Armed with modern technology, detective agencies and law officers were able to relay messages from one town to another, improving their ability to track the movements of the bandit gang. Within a year of the Great Northern raid, most of the Wild

Robert Redford (left) and Paul Newman star in *Butch Cassidy and the Sundance Kid* (1969).

Bunch had been tracked down by lawmen—and either killed or imprisoned.

TIME TO MOVE ON

Cassidy and Longabaugh managed to escape—with Longabaugh's girlfriend, Etta Place. In New York City, they shopped at Tiffany's jewelry store and again had their pictures taken. Then they boarded a boat bound for South America. The three settled in Argentina—a South American country popular with outlaws because it did not have a treaty with the United States that required them to return American criminals to their homeland.

The details of their activities in Argentina are sketchy. At first, they quietly raised cattle, sheep, and horses on a ranch in Chubot Province—far from the long arm of the American law. But in 1906, they abandoned the ranch, possibly because Pinkerton detectives had rediscovered their trail. Next they turned to banditry, robbing banks in Argentina and Chile and a payroll in Bolivia. The heists were successful, bringing the robbers tens of thousands of dollars in loot. Cassidy and Longabaugh also worked for a while in tin mines near La Paz, Bolivia. For two years they worked as day laborers in the mine—and again they left abruptly.

Sometime around 1907, Place—who had been acting as a scout in the bank robberies—returned to the United States. Longabaugh went with her to New York, where she had an operation for appendicitis (an inflamed appendix). Shortly thereafter, the two parted—some say forever. No one is certain where Etta Place went or what she did thereafter. Longabaugh returned to South America where he rejoined Cassidy.

THE END?

There are plenty of stories about the final days of Butch Cassidy and the Sundance Kid—and none of them can be proven: sometime between 1909 and 1911, Cassidy and Longabaugh died in a shoot-out with soldiers in Bolivia—or Argentina, Chile,

Leader of the bunch

Although Butch Cassidy planned many of the raids performed by the Wild Bunch, he probably wasn't the gang's leader. Harvey Logan--who was known as Kid Curry--was a hardened killer who had more authority among the band of outlaws.

or Uruguay; Cassidy shot himself in the head when he saw Sundance felled by Bolivian soldiers; Cassidy escaped to work as a soldier-for-hire in the Mexican Revolution; he changed his name to William K. Phillips and moved to Spokane, Washington, where he died in 1937.

The Bolivian shoot-out is the most widely accepted version of how the outlaws died. But nothing in army and police files at San Vicente supports the story—not even the corpses that were dug up from the local cemetery and examined.

Hole-in-the-wall hideout

The Hole-in-the-Wall was one of the Wild Bunch gang's favorite hideouts. A valley in the Wyoming wilderness, it was shielded by a mountain passage. The trail was so narrow that riders were forced to enter it single file—which discouraged many posses and lawmen from pursuing the outlaws into the area.

Sources for Further Reading

The American West, A Cultural Encyclopedia, Volumes 7 and 10. Danbury, CT: Grolier Educational Corp., 1995, pp. 1199–1201, 1691–1692.

Nash, Jay Robert. *Bloodletters and Badmen.* New York: M. Evans, 1973, pp. 114–118.

North, Mark. "To Hell You Ride, On the Trail of Butch Cassidy." *Bicycling* (October 1997), pp. 77–83.

Prassel, Frank Richard. *The Great American Outlaw, A Legacy of Fact and Fiction.* Norman, OK: University of Oklahoma Press, 1993, pp. 308–314.

Rosa, Joseph. *The Taming of the West: Age of the Gunfighter.* New York: Smithmark, 1993, pp. 69, 72.

Ross, Stewart. *Fact or Fiction: Bandits & Outlaws.* Surrey, British Columbia: Copper Beech Books, 1995, p. 39.

Steckmesser, Kent. *Western Outlaws: The "Good Badman" in Fact, Film, and Folklore.* Claremont, CA: Regina Books, 1983, pp. 115–124.

Curly Bill
(William Brocius)

Born: 1857
Died: 1882?

A number of outlaws and lawmen had reputations for being fancy shooters. Some were able to spin a pistol around their index finger, cock it, and fire. Billy the Kid and Pat Garrett were both rumored to be skilled at the spin-and-cock method—but Curly Bill was rumored to be the best.

A TOMBSTONE GUNSLINGER

Born William B. Graham in 1857, Brocius—who stood six feet tall and had curly black hair—was a cattle thief in Arizona as a young man. As a member of the Clanton-McLaury clan in Tombstone, he rustled livestock and earned a reputation as a drinking man who was easily provoked. He quickly became the enemy of **Wyatt Earp** (see entry) and his brothers. When the Earp brothers and Doc Holliday met the Clantons and McLaurys at O.K. Corral in October 1881, Brocius did not take part in the shoot-out. But that same month, he was involved in another incident.

Brocius was one of a number of cowboys who were disturbing the peace in Tombstone by racing their horses up and down the main street while firing their guns into the air. The town's sheriff, Fred White, appointed a deputy in an attempt to quiet things down. The deputy was Virgil Earp, Wyatt's brother. The troublemakers left town, but White and Earp trailed Brocius and cornered him in an alley. White asked for the outlaw's gun, and Brocius held out his six-shooter (a type of pistol) with the butt, or handle, facing the sheriff. Before White could take the gun from him, Brocius reportedly spun the gun around his index finger so that it was pointing directly at the sheriff. What happened next is the subject of debate. Some sources say the pistol went off when White tried to grab it from the outlaw. Others say Virgil Earp, who approached from behind, had startled Brocius, causing the hair-trigger of his gun to fire. Others say it was a cold-blooded act of violence. However it happened, Brocius shot Sheriff White.

Earp pistol-whipped (beat with a pistol) Brocius until he was unconscious, and then dragged him to jail. Within a few days, he was moved to Tucson, Arizona, where he was tried for the murder of White, who had died from his gunshot wound. Before dying, however, the lawman stated that the shooting had been accidental. Brocius was acquitted [found not guilty] of White's death.

MORE TROUBLE

The outlaw tangled with the law again on May 25, 1881, when an argument with lawman William Breakenridge ended in gunfire. Brocius was shot in the mouth in an incident that was described on the front page of the next day's newspaper the *Arizona Star*:

> The notorious Curly Bill, the man who murdered Marshal White at Tombstone last fall, and who has been concerned in several other desperate and lawless affrays [fights] in South Eastern Arizona, has at last been brought to grief, and there is likely to be a vacancy in the ranks of our border desperadoes. The affair occurred at Galeyville Thursday. A party of eight or nine cowboys, Curly Bill, and his partner Jim Wallace among the number, were in town enjoying themselves in their usual manner, when Sheriff Breakenridge of Tombstone, who was at Galeyville on business, happened [came] along.

Wallace made some insulting remarks to the deputy at the same time waving his revolver in an aggressive manner. Break-

Take a look at this!

Filmed on location in Santa Fe, New Mexico, *Wyatt Earp* (1994) tells the story of the tarnished lawman (played by Kevin Costner), his brothers, and his sickly friend Doc Holliday (played by Dennis Quaid, who lost forty pounds to play the role). Originally planned as a television miniseries, it also portrays Earp's early life.

Wyatt Earp, sworn enemy of Curly Bill.

enridge did not pay much attention to this gesture of aggression from Wallace but quietly turned around and left the party. Shortly after this, Brocius, who it would seem had a friendly feeling for Breakenridge, insisted that Wallace should go and find him and apologize for the insult given. Wallace never did and instead accompanied Brocius back to the saloon where the rest of the cowboys were drinking.

By this time Brocius, who had had just enough to drink to make him quarrelsome, was in one of his most dangerous moods and evidently looking to increase his record as a man killer. He started to verbally abuse Wallace, who, by the way, had some pretensions himself as a desperado and bad man generally. Wallace immediately went outside the door of the saloon, Brocius following close behind him. Just as Brocius stepped outside, Wallace, who had meanwhile drawn his revolver, fired, the bullet entering the left side of Brocius's neck and passing through, came out the right cheek, not breaking the jawbone. The town erupted in wild excitement.

SHOT TO PIECES

The outlaw's wound wasn't fatal. But his feud with Wyatt Earp probably was. Earp believed that Brocius was one of the outlaws responsible for the murder of his brother, Morgan, some years earlier. In the "Vendetta Ride" of 1882, Earp hunted down the suspected murderers. On March 27, the *Tombstone Epitaph* published an account of "one of the most desperate fights that ever took place on Arizona soil"—between Wyatt Earp and his brothers and a gang led by Curly Bill Brocius. Brocius, the article claimed, had been shot off his horse.

Wyatt Earp later described the incident in an August 1896 edition of the *San Francisco Examiner*:

We had ridden twenty-five miles over the mountains with the intention of camping at a certain spring. As we got near the place I had a presentiment [felt beforehand] that something was wrong and unlimbered [untied] my shotgun. Sure enough nine cowboys sprang up from the bank where the spring was and began firing at us. I jumped off my horse to return the fire, thinking my men would do the same, but they retreated. One of the cowboys who was trying to pump lead into me with a Winchester was a fellow named Curly Bill, a stage-robber whom I had been after for eight months, and for whom I had a warrant in my pocket. I fired both barrels of my gun into him, blowing him all to pieces.

Here's a book you might like:

The Righteous Revenge of Artemis Bonner, 1992, by Walter Dean Myers

When a young man receives a request from his aunt to punish his uncle's murderer, he quickly leaves New York City and heads West. Among the Old West towns he visits are Tombstone, Arizona; Lincoln, New Mexico; and Juarez, Mexico.

But not everyone believed that the outlaw was dead. Shortly after the killing was supposed to have taken place, the *Nugget,* an Arizona newspaper, offered a $1,000 reward to anyone who could prove that Brocius was dead. To this day, historians question whether the one-time lawman really killed Brocius. Some sources speculate that Brocius moved to Texas, where he lived as William Graham.

Sources for Further Reading

Horan, James. *The Lawmen of the Authentic Wild West.* New York: Crown, 1980, pp. 237–238, 241, 262, 267.

Nash, Jay Robert. *Bloodletters and Badmen.* New York: M. Evans, 1973, p. 84.

Nash, Jay Robert. *The Encyclopedia of World Crime.* Wilmette, IL: Crime Books, 1990, pp. 494–495.

Wyatt Earp

Born: March 19, 1848
Died: January 13, 1929

Although he's one of the most famous lawmen of the American West—best remembered for his role in the shoot-out at the O.K. Corral—Wyatt Earp spent only six of his eighty years working as a peacemaker. To this day, Earp has been branded as both a hero and a killer.

EARLY YEARS

Born in Monmouth, Illinois, Wyatt Berry Stapp Earp was one of five brothers. Wyatt had two older brothers—James C. (1841–1926) and Virgil W. (1843–1906)—and two younger siblings—Morgan (1851–1882) and Warren B. (1855–1900). The Earp boys spent most of their youth in Illinois and Iowa. As the end of the Civil War approached, the boys moved West with their parents to San Bernardino, California.

When Wyatt was twenty, he and his brother Virgil worked on a Union Pacific Railroad crew. They rejoined the rest of the Earp family, who had returned to Illinois. Wyatt soon relocated to Lamar, Missouri, where he married his first wife, Urilla Sutherland. In February of 1870, just one month after his marriage, Earp was appointed as the town's constable—his first job as an officer of the law. But Wyatt didn't stay long in Lamar. When Urilla died of typhoid fever (a deadly and contagious disease), Earp left town.

After leaving Missouri in 1871, Earp drifted from job to job in Indian Territory (present-day Oklahoma) and a number of towns in Kansas (where he reportedly forced a number of Texas gunmen who were causing trouble to back down). He worked as a police officer in Wichita, Kansas (1875–1876), and later took a post as the chief deputy of Dodge City, Kansas (1876–1877), where two other well-known lawmen, Bat and Jim Masterson, worked as his aides. From Dodge City, Earp headed for the gold rush in the Black Hills in the Dakota Territory—only to find that the area had already been nearly stripped of gold. Returning to Dodge City, he assumed the post of assistant marshal (1878–1879). During his days in Dodge City, Earp met two people who would become important figures in his life: Cecelia "Mattie" Blaylock, who would later become his second wife, and John "Doc" Holliday, a gunman who would become his lifelong friend.

TOMBSTONE

Tombstone, Arizona, had become a boomtown (a town that experiences sudden growth and prosperity) almost overnight. In 1877, Edward Schieffelin, a prospector, found silver in the area. (The town's name supposedly came from a friend of Schieffelin's who warned the prospector that instead of a mine, he'd find a tombstone.) Schieffelin found a motherlode (principal source or supply) of silver that eventually yielded millions of dollars in silver. Soon, the town was filled with fortune-seeking miners—as well as con artists, claim jumpers, gamblers, and gunmen. A haven for outlaws, the area often erupted with gunfights and riots. To the rest of the country, Tombstone represented chaos and lawlessness—and every other negative stereotype of the Wild West.

In December of 1879, Wyatt and Mattie arrived in Tombstone, and were soon joined by Wyatt's brothers James, Morgan, Virgil, and Warren. The following year, Virgil was appointed town marshal, and he sometimes called on Wyatt to serve as his deputy. A hard-core gambler, Wyatt also worked as a guard in the very successful Oriental Saloon.

Tombstone troublemakers

At the time of the gunfight at O.K. Corral, Tombstone, Arizona, had a population of 10,000—and a reputation for chaos. The town remained a lawless place even after the feud between the Earps and the Clanton-McLaury gang was over. Less than one year after the shoot-out, on May 3, 1882, President Chester Arthur (1829–1886) issued a proclamation stating that "it has become impracticable to enforce by the ordinary course of judicial proceedings the laws of the United States" in Tombstone. He urged the trouble-makers to "retire peacefully to their respective abodes." President Arthur was threatening Tombstone with martial law—a state of emergency in which the military takes over law enforcement.

Never a Sheriff

Wyatt Earp was never a full sheriff in Tombstone, Dodge City-- or anywhere else, for that matter.

Doc Holliday
(1851 or 1852–1887)

On his way to fight the Clanton-McLaury gang with his brothers at the O.K. Corral, Wyatt Earp tried to tell his friend, Doc Holliday, that he shouldn't join the fight. Holliday didn't listen, and received a gunshot in the hip while fighting with the Earp brothers. Although sometimes an embarrassment to the lawmaker, Holliday stood by Earp through difficult times.

John Henry Holliday was born to a genteel southern family in Griffin, Georgia, in 1851 or 1852. His father was a major in the Confederate Army during the Civil War (1861–1865). When Holliday was eleven years old, his family moved to Valdosta, Georgia, and he left home about five years later. He enrolled at a college of dental surgery on the East Coast, and at the age of twenty, set up a practice in Atlanta, Georgia. Holliday's profession as a dentist earned him the nickname "Doc." Easily angered, he earned a reputation as a dangerous man. It was said that he was well-drilled (skilled) in the art of dentistry, but for those who doubted his ability, he would drill (shoot) them for free.

Holliday suffered pulmonary tuberculosis (a deadly disease that affects the lungs), the disease that took his mother's life. A sickly man throughout his life, he was thin and weak, and often fell into terrible coughing fits. Bat Masterson, a lawman who was an acquaintance of Holliday's, said this about him: "Physically, Doc Holliday was a weakling who could not have whipped a healthy fifteen-year-old boy in a fight."

As his health grew worse, Holliday was forced to leave Georgia for a drier climate. A

Wyatt brothers

Wyatt's older brother Virgil was considered to be the leader of the Earp brothers during their stay in Tombstone, Arizona. His younger brother Morgan had a reputation as the hothead in the family.

By 1881, the Earps were involved in a feud with a gang of outlaws led by Joseph Isiah "Ike" Clanton. Operating from their ranches west of town, on the San Pedro River, the Clantons—Ike and his younger brother Billy—and the McLaury brothers—Tom and Frank—rustled cattle and robbed stagecoaches in the area. The Clantons and McLaurys were a powerful gang that wanted to rid Tombstone of the Earp brothers, who threatened their livelihood.

THE GUNFIGHT AT O.K. CORRAL

It was simply a matter of time before the feud between the Clanton-McLaury gang and the Earp brothers ended in violence. Frank McLaury challenged Morgan Earp to a shoot-out,

gambler and a heavy drinker, he drifted from one town to another. In Texas, he reportedly killed for the first time. He also stopped in a number of western boomtowns, including Tucson, Tombstone, and Dodge City—where he probably met and befriended Wyatt Earp. Historians have never been able to explain Earp's loyalty to Holliday—although some speculate that Holliday saved the lawman's life sometime during their stay in Dodge City.

Earp was impressed by Holliday's ability to handle a gun. He claimed that the dentist was "the nerviest, speediest, deadliest man with a six-gun that I ever knew." But he wasn't a man to argue with. Bat Masterson said that Holliday had "a mean disposition and an ungovernable temper, and under the influence of liquor was a most dangerous man." The list of his dangerous activities was long. In Las Vegas, New Mexico, he killed a man in a saloon fight. In another fight, he killed a bartender. Holliday was also suspected of stagecoach and train robbery. Free on bail at the time of the O.K. Corral gunfight, Holliday later helped the Earps to track down and kill two men suspected of the murder of Morgan Earp.

Liquor contributed to Holliday's poor health. Weakened by alcoholism, he fell into uncontrollable coughing fits that left him helpless. In May of 1887—less than six years after the gunfight at O.K. Corral—he entered a hospital in Glenwood Springs, Colorado. Six months later, as the story goes, he propped himself up in bed and yelled to a nurse, "Dammit, put them back on." Holliday wanted to die *with his boots on.* But the nurse was too late. At 10 A.M. on November 8, 1887, Doc Holliday died. Although he was in his mid-thirties, his illness had made him look like a man in his eighties.

but Earp refused. But when Ike Clanton got into an argument with Doc Holliday in a saloon on the afternoon of October 25, 1881, he set in motion a series of events that would lead to a showdown—the gunfight at O.K. Corral.

The morning after the argument, Ike Clanton was still angry. He made threats against the Earps and he waved a gun in town. Virgil Earp, the town marshal, deputized his brothers Wyatt and Morgan, as well as Doc Holliday. Then he arrested Clanton for carrying guns within the city limits. Clanton was taken to court and fined. Outside the courthouse, Wyatt and Tom McLaury broke into an argument—which ended when Earp "buffaloed" McLaury by hitting him on the side of his head with a pistol.

Inside the O.K. Corral
at Tombstone, Arizona.

Later that day, the Earps learned that the Clantons and McLaurys were gathered near the O.K. Corral. Convinced that a shoot-out was in the making, the Earp brothers headed to a vacant lot on Fremont Street where the outlaws awaited them. Doc Holliday joined the Earps, although Wyatt had tried to discourage him from joining the fight.

The shoot-out was short but brutal. In very little time—somewhere between thirty seconds and three minutes—three of the eight men involved were dead. Among the dead were Frank and Tom McLaury, and nineteen-year-old Billy Clanton, who had wounds in his chest, head, and wrist. Of the four lawmen involved, only Wyatt Earp was uninjured. Ike Clanton was the only other man to escape without being shot. Clanton had run into Fly's photographic studio when the shooting began.

Beyond O.K.

Although the town had been rid of three troublesome outlaws, the people of Tombstone were not happy about the violent events of October 26. Many believed that the gunfight was murder disguised as crime fighting. Immediately after the shoot-out, town sheriff John E. Behan issued warrants for the arrest of Wyatt Earp and Doc Holliday. Justice of the Peace Wells Spicer reviewed the case for thirty days, and finally decided that there was not enough evidence to charge Earp and Holliday with murder. They were released. Although Virgil Earp was not arrested, he was dismissed from his duties as town marshal and criticized for having deputized his brothers.

The violence was far from over. On November 28—just over one month after the gunfight—Virgil was ambushed on his way into the Oriental Saloon. Shot by an unidentified gunman, he was disabled for life. In March of 1882, Morgan was shot and killed. Wyatt and his brother Warren tracked and killed a number of men they believed to be responsible for the shootings.

Now labeled a murderer, Wyatt fled first to Colorado and then to assorted boomtowns in the West—from Idaho to Arizona and Alaska. In 1888, after Mattie Earp died, he married his third wife (and longtime girlfriend) Josephine Sarah Marcus. Wyatt eventually settled in California, where he became a familiar figure at the horse racing tracks. He mingled with movie stars and lived to a ripe old age. He died on January 13, 1929, at the age of eighty—having outlived every one of his four brothers.

Waxed pockets

A tall, well-groomed man who never left home without his coat and tie, Wyatt Earp didn't wear the traditional gun belt and holster. Instead, he had tailor-made waxed pockets in his suit coat that allowed him to remove the gun easily.

Sources for Further Reading

The American West, A Cultural Encyclopedia, Volumes 3 and 8. Danbury, CT: Grolier Educational Corp., 1995, pp. 468–471, 1345.

"Brave, Courageous and Bold." *New York Times Book Review* (November 9, 1997), p. 72.

Nash, Jay Robert. *Bloodletters and Badmen.* New York: M. Evans, 1973, pp. 423–428.

Rosa, Joseph. *The Taming of the West: Age of the Gunfighter.* New York: Smithmark, 1993, pp. 120–121, 128, 134, 179–180, 184–185.

Ross, Stewart. *Fact or Fiction: Bandits & Outlaws.* Surrey, British Columbia: Copper Beech Books, 1995, pp. 24–25.

Wukovits, John. *The Gunslingers.* Broomall, PA: Chelsea House, 1997, pp. 37–39.

Jesse James

Born: September 5, 1847
Died: April 3, 1882
AKA: "Dingus," J. D. Howard

*Together with his brother Frank, Jesse James made a career
out of robbing banks and trains. Although he was a ruthless
killer, he was also a religious family man. Even before he
was murdered by a gang-member turned-traitor, the legend
of Jesse James was larger than life.*

A PREACHER'S SON

Zerelda Cole was just sixteen when she left a Catholic
convent to marry Robert James, a well-educated Baptist minister. The couple left Kentucky in the early 1840s to try their
luck at running a small farm in Clay County, Missouri, about
twenty miles northwest of Kansas City. The couple's first son,
Alexander Franklin James, was born in 1843. Nearly five
years later, on September 5, 1847, Jesse Woodson James was
born.

Robert James left his family to join the California gold rush.
Jesse, who was three years old at the time, never saw his father
again. A few weeks after he arrived in California to seek his fortune, Robert James died of pneumonia, at the age of twenty-
six. Zerelda soon remarried, but quickly divorced her fifty- year-
old second husband. She gave her boys a religious upbringing,
and in 1857 married her third husband, Reuben Samuel, who
was a farmer and doctor.

AN UNCIVIL WAR

Frank and Jesse were teenagers when the Civil War erupted in 1861—the same year that Kansas became a state. It was also a time of brutal border wars between Kansas "Red Legs" or "Jayhawkers"—who opposed slavery—and Missouri "Bushwackers"—who were in favor of continuing the practice of slavery. Both sides formed guerrilla forces, which employed "irregular" methods of warfare such as violent surprise attacks.

The James brothers had no trouble choosing sides. Their family owned several black slaves, and they were committed to supporting the Confederacy. (The Confederacy was a group of eleven pro-slavery Southern states that broke away from the Union in 1860–1861 to form their own government.) Frank, who had enlisted in the Confederate army, was jailed by Federal militia for taking part in the Confederate cause. He was released from prison after he signed an oath pledging his loyalty to the Union—a promise he did not intend to keep.

As the Civil War raged, Frank, and later Jesse, took part in the vicious guerrilla (outlaw soldier) battles between Confederate and Union supporters. Frank joined the army of William Clarke Quantrill, a Southern guerrilla leader, and participated in a bloody raid on Lawrence, Kansas, on August 20, 1863. About one year later, Jesse joined the guerrilla band under one of Quantrill's lieutenants, "Bloody Bill" Anderson. Jesse soon became an expert marksman and horseback rider. By his eighteenth birthday, he had participated in many violent raids on anti-slavery towns. These raids left countless Union soldiers dead. At Centralia, Missouri, in 1864, for example, Jesse and other Confederate guerrillas murdered dozens of unarmed Union soldiers.

FALSE PARDON

At the end of the Civil War, Southern troops were pardoned. But guerrilla fighters were tracked and killed. The James brothers continued to live as hunted outlaws until 1865, when the government offered all guerrilla soldiers amnesty (pardon). According to legend, on April 1, 1865, Frank and Jesse James rode into the small town of Lexington, Missouri, waving the white flag of surrender. They were met by a group of cavalry soldiers who ignored their attempt to surrender and opened fire on the former guerrillas. Both James brothers managed to escape—although Jesse was shot in the chest and nearly died.

Weak and wounded, Jesse was helped back to his family by Southern sympathizers. Because of their strong support of the Confederate cause, Zerelda and Reuben Samuel had been forced to leave Missouri for Nebraska. But Jesse, who was afraid that he might die, insisted that the family return to its native state. He is said to have vowed, "I don't want to die in a Northern state." In the fall of 1865 he was brought by covered wagon back to Clay County, where his uncle, John Mimms, ran a boardinghouse. Jesse's cousin, also named Zerelda, helped to nurse him back to health. After a nine-year engagement, Jesse married Zerelda—or "Zee," as she was called.

A NEW CAREER

At eight o'clock on the morning of February 13, 1866, four men strolled into the Clay County Savings and Loan Bank in Liberty, Missouri. Six others stayed outside on their horses. Minutes later the men—including Frank James and his cousin Cole Younger—rode out of town with a wheat sack filled with $60,000 in bonds and currency. One man was dead. The Clay County heist was the first bank robbery committed by the James-Younger gang. But it was far from the last. For more than ten years, the James boys and their cousins, the Younger brothers—Cole, James, John, and Robert—were the central figures in a criminal gang that made off with hundreds of thousands of dollars in stolen goods.

The gang covered a lot of territory, robbing banks in seven states: Arkansas, Iowa, Kentucky, Minnesota, Missouri, Texas, and West Virginia. Using some of the skills they had learned as

Popular reading material

The public loved to read about the real and fictional exploits of Jesse James and his gang. Their adventures were written up in books, dime novels and weeklies (newspapers). In just two years (between 1901 and 1903), the Street and Smith publishing house sold *six million* copies of 121 Jesse James novels.

Will the real Jesse James please stand up!

A number of people believe that Jesse James faked his own death. After the outlaw's supposed corpse was exhumed (dug up) and examined, scientists determined that DNA extracted from the corpse's hair was nearly identical to that of the outlaw's sister's descendants. But that didn't stop would-be relatives from claiming that James did not die in Missouri at the hands of Bob Ford.

Some claimed that James had lived out his days in Granbury, Texas—where he died at the age of 103. In the 1920s and 1930s, circuses often staged sideshows featuring the "real" Jesse James. And for years, the descendants of J. Frank Dalton have claimed that their bearded ancestor was, in fact, Jesse James. Supporting their claim was a 1951 autopsy report that identifies Dalton as the infamous gunslinger. The report states that the corpse of Dalton is missing the tip of the left forefinger. (During the Civil War, James accidentally shot off the tip of his finger.) Dalton's body also contained more than thirty bullet wounds. Most of the evidence, however, relied on statements from friends and family who claimed to have overheard the old Texan boast that he was the former outlaw.

More recently, a Texas woman named Betty Dorsett Duke entered her claim as the great-

Imposters

After the Northfield disaster, Frank and Jesse James disappeared into the Dakota Territory. They sometimes posed as law officers--and told several citizens that *they* were going to capture the James boys.

guerrilla fighters, the outlaws arrived at a successful formula for robbery. They planned their hits carefully and attacked suddenly and violently. And they always plotted their escape before they struck their targets. Most years, the gang staged only one or two robberies, which left the James brothers plenty of time to live peacefully as farmers.

In 1873, the gang added train robbery—a relatively new and very profitable form of robbery—to its growing list of illegal activities. They pulled off their first theft by loosening a rail at a blind curve in order to stop the train. The robbers made off with only $2,000. But future train robberies would be more profitable. One of the gang's most successful robberies took place in 1875, when the James brothers and seven others robbed the Missouri-Pacific Express train of $75,000.

SHOWDOWN IN NORTHFIELD

The gang's next target was the First National Bank in Northfield, Minnesota. On August 7, 1876, eight members of the gang

granddaughter of Jesse James. Her great-grandfather, a farmer named James Lafayette Courtney, lived in Texas to the ripe old age of ninety-six. After he died on April 14, 1943, he was buried in a cemetery in Falls County. The evidence Duke presents was surprising:

- A portrait of James Lafayette Courtney was surprisingly similar to a famous photograph of Jesse James that was taken in Nebraska in 1866.

- Many photos of Courtney showed him with his left hand curled in. Jesse James reportedly used the same pose to hide his injured finger.

- A photograph of Courtney's mother, Dianah Andruss Courtney, appeared to be identical to a photo of Jesse's mother, Zerelda James Samuel. Like Zerelda Samuels, Dianah Courtney's left arm ended at the elbow.

- Many other Courtney family photographs resembled photographs of Jesse's relatives.

- Courtney's diary mentioned Bill Wilkerson, a member of the James gang. And Wilkerson's brother sometimes lived with the Courtneys.

- Courtney had a lot of money for a farmer. He bought a farm for every one of his eight children. And he paid cash.

rode into the peaceful Minnesota farming town. The group included both James brothers and three of their cousins—Bob, Cole, and Jim Younger—as well as Charlie Pitts, Clell Miller, and Bill Chadwell. They all wore new boots and well-pressed suits, and rode handsome, well-kept horses.

The robbery didn't go well from the start. The bank teller claimed the safe was time-locked and couldn't be opened. (As it turned out, the safe was *open*—but the robbers hadn't looked.) Two men in the street had noticed the activity by the bank, and started shouting to alert the townspeople. Gunfire broke out inside the bank, and the outlaws were fired on by citizens when they abandoned the heist. Miller and Chadwell were shot dead in the street, and most of the others were wounded.

Followed by an angry posse (a group of people with legal authority to capture criminals), the surviving members of the gang split up. Frank and Jesse struck out together, while Pitts joined the three Younger brothers. Two weeks later, a posse caught up with the Youngers, and a shoot-out followed. Pitts was killed and the three brothers were captured. The Younger

Bob Ford, killer of
Jesse James.

boys were all wounded (Cole had been hit by eleven bullets), but they recovered and were each sentenced to life in prison.

THE SECOND JAMES GANG

Frank and Jesse James were the only gang members who weren't dead or in prison. For three years they laid low. They lived in Nashville, Tennessee, and hid their identities by taking new names. Frank James and his wife lived as the Woodsons, while Jesse and Zee called themselves the Howards. But by October 1879, the James brothers returned to Missouri and organized a new gang that specialized in train robbery. The gang included Tucker Basham, Wood Hite, Dick Liddel, Ed Miller (who was Clell's brother), and Bill Ryan.

The gang's first hit was successful. On October 7, 1879, it robbed a train near Glendale, Missouri, of $35,000. For two years gang members continued to rob and kill, but the second James gang soon began to fall apart. They were ruthlessly pursued by lawmen and hired detectives. The gang's new members were outsiders who weren't loyal family members, as the Youngers had been. They fought among themselves over the loot they had stolen. And they betrayed one another.

THE MAN WHO SHOT JESSE JAMES

Charles Ford and his brother Robert were two new recruits who sometimes accompanied the James gang on their raids. They disliked Jesse and argued with him. And they had no problem planning to stake their claim to the $10,000 reward that Thomas T. Crittenden, the governor of Missouri, had offered for the capture and conviction of Jesse James.

In the spring of 1882, the James brothers and the Fords were the only living gang members who had escaped capture. On April 3, the Fords met Jesse at his home in St. Joseph, Missouri, to plan another robbery. Jesse's wife Zee fixed breakfast

An American Robin Hood

Many people saw Jesse James as a hero. In a popular song composed shortly after his death, Jesse's life was glorified:

Jesse James was a lad who killed many a man.

He robbed the Glendale train.

He stole from the rich and he gave to the poor,

He'd a hand and a heart and a brain.

Although many people viewed Jesse James as a modern-day Robin Hood, there is no real evidence that he gave to the poor. But there were plenty of unconfirmed stories that portray him as a brave and kind gentleman thief. In one such story, James gives a widow $3,000 to prevent a banker from taking over her run-down cabin. The widow pays the banker and regains ownership of her home. A few miles from the widow's cabin, James robs the banker of the $3,000 and his watch, and rides away laughing to himself. It's possible that James was the Robin Hood of this story. Then again, versions of the story have been told about a number of other outlaws—including Butch Cassidy, who told it about himself.

Jesse's choice of targets probably contributed to his popularity. The James gangs robbed from banks and railroad companies, both of which were unpopular among poor country dwellers. Many viewed banking houses as crooked institutions. Railroad companies were the enemy of poor farmers, who believed they were run by robber barons who cheated honest people out of their property.

for them. Jesse and Zee's son, Jesse Jr. and Mary, their daughter, played outside. After breakfast, Jesse stood on a chair to straighten a picture on the wall. Before he stepped on the chair, he removed his jacket—and both gun belts.

Standing about six feet from the outlaw, Bob Ford shot him in the back of the head. Jesse James was dead at the age of thirty-four. When Zee ran into the room, Ford claimed that the gun—a revolver that Jesse had given him a few days earlier—had gone off accidentally.

Two weeks after the shooting, Ford brothers were convicted of murder and sentenced to death. Hours later, Governor Crittenden issued a pardon that spared their lives. The governor denied that he had plotted with Robert Ford—who received a little over $600 of the $10,000 reward. Having lost the respect of an entire nation for shooting an unarmed man in the back, he

The house in St. Louis, Missouri, where Jesse James was killed on April 3, 1882, is a popular tourist attraction.

was remembered in a ballad (a popular song) that was composed shortly after Jesse's death. One verse of the song went:

It was Robert Ford, that dirty little coward,
I wonder how he does feel,
For he ate of Jesse's bread and he slept in Jesse's bed,
Then he laid Jesse James in his grave.

THE END OF THE OUTLAWS

Within a few months of his brother's death, on October 5, 1882, Frank James surrendered to the authorities. He was a beaten man who was sick of running. Asked why he had surrendered, he said, "I was tired of an outlaw's life. I have been hunted for twenty-one years. I have literally lived in the saddle. I have never known a day of perfect peace." In three separate trials for murder, robbery, and armed robbery, Frank James was tried and set free. He never served a prison sentence for his crimes, and led a peaceful life on the family farm. He died on February 18, 1915, in the room in which he had been born. He was seventy-two years old.

Nearly twenty years after Jesse's death, Jim and Cole Younger were paroled from prison. They had served almost twenty-five years when they were released on July 11, 1901. Their brother, Bob, had died of tuberculosis (a disease that affects the lungs) while still in prison. One year after their release, Jim Younger committed suicide. Cole made a career giving lectures about the evils of crime. He died at the age of seventy-two, bearing the scars of twenty bullet wounds.

Charles Ford committed suicide in 1884. Jesse's killer, Robert Ford, performed for a while in traveling shows such as *The Outlaws of Missouri* and *How I Killed Jesse James.* He eventually became a saloonkeeper in Creede, Colorado. There, his past caught up with him. Ed Kelly, a relative of the Youngers, shot Ford to death during a quarrel in 1892.

Here's a book you might like:

Mamaw, 1988, by Susan Dodd

Zerelda Samuel—the mother of the infamous James boys, known as Mamaw—is raised in a convent, marries at sixteen, rescues one husband from hanging, loses her hand to a Pinkerton bomb meant for her sons, and then watches as her sons are hunted down.

Sources for Further Reading

The American West, A Cultural Encyclopedia, Volume 5. Danbury, CT: Grolier Educational Corp., 1995, pp. 822–826.

Dingus, Anne. "Body of Evidence." *Texas Monthly* (August 1997), p. 22+.

Nash, Jay Robert. *Bloodletters and Badmen.* New York: M. Evans, 1973, pp. 265–285.

Prassel, Frank Richard. *The Great American Outlaw, A Legacy of Fact and Fiction.* Norman, OK: University of Oklahoma Press, 1993, pp. 125–138.

Rosa, Joseph. *The Taming of the West: Age of the Gunfighter.* New York: Smithmark, 1993, pp. 40–45.

Son or daughter?

After the Northfield disaster, Frank James and his wife Annie called themselves Mr. and Mrs. B. J. Woodson. The couple had a son, Robert Franklin James. To throw his enemies off his trail, the "Woodsons" dressed their son as a girl and called him Mary.

Ross, Stewart. *Fact or Fiction: Bandits & Outlaws.* Surrey, British Columbia: Copper Beech Books, 1995, pp. 38–39.

Steckmesser, Kent. *Western Outlaws: The "Good Badman" in Fact, Film, and Folklore.* Claremont, CA: Regina Books, 1983, pp. 43–68.

Vandome, Nick. *Crimes and Criminals.* New York: Chambers, 1992, pp. 119–120.

Belle Starr
(Myra Belle Shirley)

Born: February 5, 1848
Died: February 3, 1889

Sometimes called the female Jesse James, Belle Starr was an expert rider and a good shot. A foul-tempered cattle and horse thief, she lived with a number of outlaws and earned a reputation as a Bandit Queen in Texas and the Indian Territory.

BORDER WARS AND BANDITRY

Myra Belle Shirley was born in a log cabin near Carthage, Missouri, in 1848. Her father, a farmer and tavern owner, came from a wealthy and aristocratic (socially exclusive) Virginia family. At the age of eight, Belle enrolled in the Carthage Female Academy, where she attended classes through the eighth grade. Because the Kansas-Missouri border had become a battleground for people who were fighting over slavery, Belle's father decided to move his family away from the violence—to Scyene, Texas, not far from Dallas.

Several years after her family moved to Texas—after the Civil War had ended—Belle met an outlaw named Cole Younger, a former Confederate guerrilla (outlaw soldier), who was the cousin of Jesse James and a member of the Younger-James gang. Younger was hiding from the law following a Missouri bank robbery. Belle ran away with Younger in 1866, and the two lived together in a cabin on the Oklahoma Strip. Younger eventually rejoined his brothers and the rest of the

Western outlaw Belle Starr on horseback.

James gang. Shortly after he left, Belle had a daughter, Pearl. Most historians assume that Younger was Pearl's father.

Belle soon had a son, Edward, whose father was another outlaw, Jim Reed. Belle and Reed left Texas in 1869 because lawmen were on their trail. In California, near the North Canadian River, they pulled a robbery. According to some sources, they forced a prospector to tell them where he had hidden a large stash of gold. In other reports, they tortured a Creek Indian chief into telling them where his tribe's government subsidy (a grant of money) was hidden. In any case, Belle and Reed left California $30,000 richer.

Returning to Texas, Belle enjoyed her new-found wealth. She sometimes wore velvet dresses, shiny boots, and feathered hats—and often strapped a gun belt over her skirt. And she rode an expensive black race-horse named Venus (side-saddle, as women of that era were expected to). Reed was killed in a gun fight in August of 1874, and Belle reportedly refused to identify his body so that his killer would not be able to collect the reward that had been offered for his capture.

Mrs. Sam Starr

After Reed's death, Belle left her two children with her mother and helped to run a horse- and cattle-stealing ring in the Indian Territory. She lived briefly with a Native American rustler named Blue Duck, and then in 1880 met and married Sam Starr, a Cherokee outlaw who was four years her junior. Married according to Cherokee custom, Belle took an oath of allegiance to the Cherokee Nation. She kept the Starr name throughout the rest of her life.

The Starrs settled near the Canadian River, in an area she named Younger's Bend—in memory of her former love, Cole Younger. Housing outlaws in guest rooms, the couple ran a hideout for fugitives. Jesse James reportedly stayed with the Starrs following a train robbery in 1881.

Three years after they were married, Starr and Belle were both tried for horse theft by Isaac Parker—the so-called "hanging judge." Starr was sentenced to less than one year in prison. Belle—whom Parker called the "leader of a notorious band of horse thieves"—enjoyed a reputation in the newspapers as "the petticoat of the planes" and "the lady desperado." Belle played up her role as the Lady Bandit, posing for numerous pictures before serving time in a prison in Detroit, Michigan.

Released from prison, the Starrs returned to Younger's Bend and resumed their careers as horse and cattle rustlers. After they were arrested by U.S. marshals in 1886 they were tried. Judge Parker released the couple because there was not enough evidence to convict them of theft. But their freedom was short-lived. Sam Starr was killed later that year by a Native American police officer. (According to some sources, the shooting took place at a dance. Others claim that Sam and one of the officers who arrested him got into a barroom fight that left both men dead.)

A LEGEND IN THE MAKING

After Starr's death, Belle remained at Younger's Bend and became involved with Jim July, a Creek Indian who was wanted for robbery. A few months after the two were married, in 1889, Belle was killed in an ambush. No one is sure who killed her—although there are several theories concerning her killer's motives and identity. Some believed that an angry former lover was responsible for the killing. Others believed the culprit to be a neighbor named Edgar Watson, who had quarreled with her about land. Some suspected Belle's eighteen-year-old son, Edward, who had a difficult relationship with his mother. At the time, R. P. Vann—a neighbor and former member of the Indian police—suggested that Edward had a motive in the killing: "Among the people in the Belle Starr country," Vann reported, "it is commonly accepted belief that there were incestuous relations [sexual relations between people who are related] between Belle and her son and that she complicated this with extreme sadism [delight in cruelty]." Some historians have concluded that—given the surroundings—Belle must have seen her shooter. Although a neighbor found her before she died, she never named her killer.

Belle was buried at Younger's Bend, in a Cherokee ceremony: jewelry was laid in her coffin and a revolver (possibly one given to her by Cole Younger) was placed at her hand. Her daughter, Pearl, had a monument placed at the grave. It was inscribed with the words:

Shed not for her the bitter tear,
Nor give the heart to vain [useless] regret,
'Tis but the casket that lies here,
The gem that fills it sparkles yet.

Shortly after Belle was buried, her grave was robbed. Within three years, Jim July died in an Arkansas jail.

Thanks to a New York author, Belle Starr became a legend soon after she died. *Belle Starr, the Bandit Queen, or the Female Jesse James: A Full and Authentic History of the Dashing Female Highwayman,* by Richard Fox (a dime-novel author), was billed as the authentic biography of the woman rustler. In reality, it was a sensationalized adventure tale that had little to do with the truth. Fox painted a heroic picture of Belle: "Of all women . . . the universe produced none more remarkable than Belle Starr, the Bandit Queen. Her character was a combination of the very worst as well as some of the very best traits of her sex. She was more amorous [loving] than Anthony's mistress, more relentless [harsh] than Pharaoh's daughter, and braver than Joan of Arc." And Fox didn't stop there. He made up diary entries that were supposed to have been written by the notorious Bandit Queen.

Confederate supporters

Belle's twin brother, Ed, was reportedly a captain in the Confederate Army, serving under the notorious outlaw leader William Clarke "Bloody Bill" Quantrill. Hunted by Union troops, Ed was killed. Belle also worked for the Confederate "irregulars": she was arrested as a Confederate courier.

Sources for Further Reading

The American West, A Cultural Encyclopedia, Volume 9. Danbury, CT: Grolier Educational Corp., 1995, pp. 1514–1516.

Bruns, Roger. *The Bandit Kings from Jesse James to Pretty Boy Floyd.* New York: Crown, 1995, pp. 166, 217.

Horan, James. *The Lawmen of the Authentic Wild West.* New York: Crown, 1980, p. 171.

Lewis, Jon E. *The Mammoth Book of the West.* New York: Carroll & Graf, 1996, pp. 334–335.

Nash, Jay Robert. *Bloodletters and Badmen.* New York: M. Evans, 1973, pp. 527–529.

O'Neal, Bill. *Encyclopedia of Western Gunfighters.* Norman, OK: University of Oklahoma Press, 1979, pp. 260–261, 297–298, 346–347.

Pirotta, Saviour. *The Wild, Wild West.* Austin, TX: Raintree Steck-Vaughn, 1997, pp. 28–29.

Prassel, Frank Richard. *The Great American Outlaw, A Legacy of Fact and Fiction.* Norman, OK: University of Oklahoma Press, 1993, pp. 188–190, 227–229.

The children of Belle Starr

Edward Reed, the son of Belle Starr and outlaw Jim Reed, was convicted of bootlegging and later served a term as a deputy federal marshal. He was killed in a barroom fight in 1896. Belle's daughter, Pearl, became a well-known prostitute at Fort Smith, Arkansas. She died in 1925.

Ross, Stewart. *Fact or Fiction: Cowboys.* Surrey, British Columbia: Copper Beech, 1995, p. 23.

Sifakis, Carl. *The Encyclopedia of American Crime.* New York: Facts on File, 1982, pp. 683–685.

Ward, Geoffrey. *The West, An Illustrated History.* Boston: Little, Brown, 1996, p. 356.

Dallas Stoudenmire

Born: December 11, 1845
Died: September 18, 1882

A former Texas Ranger, Dallas Stoudenmire began his career as a well-respected U.S. marshal, but he soon acquired a reputation for drinking too much and shooting too freely. He has been remembered as one of the most sensational lawmen of the West— and as a man who sometimes stood on the wrong side of the law.

A CONFEDERATE RANGER

A Southerner by birth, Dallas Stoudenmire was born in 1845 in Aberfoil, Alabama. He grew up in a large family, and when the Civil War broke out in 1861, he didn't wait long to join the fighting. Stoudenmire is reported to have joined the Confederate army in 1862, when he was just sixteen years old. (The Confederate army fought for the eleven Southern states that broke away from the Union in order to form their own government.) Although he received many severe wounds, he survived the war and later settled in Texas. He tried his luck—very briefly—as a farmer near Columbus, Texas.

Stoudenmire joined the Frontier Battalion of the Texas Rangers, where he soon became known as a man who was fearless to a fault—and who was easily provoked to violence and showed no remorse for killing. An imposing man who stood over six feet tall, he was feared by the outlaws he pursued—as well as the citizens he protected.

EL PASO'S MURDEROUS MARSHAL

By the time he left the Texas Rangers, Stoudenmire had a reputation as a gunslinger who shot first and asked questions later. He became the marshal of Socorro, New Mexico, where he participated in a number of gun-fights—some of which led people to question which side of the law he represented. In 1881 he returned to Texas, presumably at the request of his brother-in-law, Samuel "Doc" Cummings, owner of the city's finest restaurant, the Globe. He served imported food and advertised "No dust, no noise, no flies." Having married Stoudenmire's sister in Columbus, Texas, Cummings farmed in the panhandle, ran a hotel in San Marcial, New Mexico, and then traveled by stagecoach to El Paso—a town he'd never even visited. He arrived there on Christmas Eve of 1880.

The El Paso that Cummings and Stoudenmire encountered was a lawless and violent boomtown (a town that experiences sudden growth and prosperity). The town's mayor, Solomon Schutz, showed more concern for his personal interests than for El Paso's welfare, and city marshals—who seldom stayed in office long—had a difficult time attempting to maintain law and order within the city limits. Adding to the border town's troubles were frequent and ongoing disputes between Mexicans and Americans.

After his predecessor (the former marshal) was forced to resign, Stoudenmire became marshal of El Paso on April 11, 1881. Involved in two shoot-outs within days of his appointment, he quickly made a number of enemies. But he also had his supporters. El Paso's city leaders were pleased with his ability to intimidate the town's many criminals.

During his brief term in office, Stoudenmire developed a personal feud with the wealthy Manning brothers—George, Frank, and Jim. The Mannings owned one of the state's largest cattle ranches and controlled most of the town's thriving saloon business. George Manning, was a well-respected doctor in El Paso. Adding fuel to the feud was a shoot-out between Stoudenmire and John Hale, an associate of the Manning brothers. Stoudenmire gunned down Hale. He also shot an innocent bystander and George Campbell—a former city marshal and friend of the Mannings. Campbell protested during the gunfight that he was not involved in the dispute and claimed, on his deathbed, that the marshal had murdered him.

A FAILED AMBUSH

Stoudenmire and Cummings were frequently attacked, and they believed the Mannings had hired assassins to kill them. On April 17, 1882, Bill Johnson—who had resigned as city marshal before Stoudenmire arrived—attempted to ambush the two lawmen. Hiding behind a pile of bricks that were to be used in the construction of the State National Bank, he waited for his targets to pass on their nightly rounds. When Stoudenmire and Cummings approached, he fired, missed, and was shot dead by his intended victims. Stoudenmire was then wounded in the heel by one of a group of shooters who were hiding across the street. Following the shooting, he retreated to a Texas Ranger camp. Stoudenmire returned to El Paso one week later to find the town divided for and against him. Although he blamed the Manning brothers for the incident, he had no evidence that tied them to the attack.

DEAD DEPUTY

In February 1882, Stoudenmire deputized Cummings in order to help a Kansas sheriff who was trailing a rapist to Chihuahua, Mexico. When Cummings returned, both Stoudenmire and his deputy, James Gillett, were ill with the flu—leaving Cummings in charge. Later that month, Stoudenmire left town on a honeymoon with his new wife, Isabella Sherrington. With Gillett still ill, Cummings continued on as the town's deputy.

Before Stoudenmire returned, Cummings was shot dead at the Coliseum saloon. Jim Manning was the shooter. Although a judge later ruled that Manning had acted in self-defense, the killing raised a number of questions. The deputy's corpse had two bullet wounds and a fractured skull. Although Manning claimed to have shot twice, only one of the cartridges in his pis-

---

Ready, set, jump!

When El Paso city council members gathered to fire Stoudenmire from his post as marshal, they were afraid of how the lawman might react. Some of the councilmen sat on window sills in front of open windows—to make sure they could escape in case the marshal flew into a rage.

Fighting like the very devil

The Texas Rangers were established long before Dallas Stoudenmire was even born. Texas was colonized in 1823 by Stephen Austin (1793–1836), who ordered a group of "rangers" to handle hostile Mexican and Native American raiders. John S. "Rip" Ford, a well known Texas Ranger, once boasted that a ranger was required to "ride like a Mexican, trail like an Indian, shoot like a Tennessean, and fight like the very devil."

Within twelve years, the Texas Rangers became official law enforcers. They also fought in the Texas War of Independence (1835) and in the Mexican War (1846–1848). When the group broke up during the Civil War (1861–1865), many former rangers fought in the Confederate army. By 1874, the rangers were reorganized to combat outlaw gangs, livestock rustlers, stagecoach and bank robbers, and other criminals.

Never governed by military or local laws, Texas Rangers were able to travel freely across the entire state. While most rangers in the Old West were employed in areas that had no local government, Texas Rangers were called on when local officers were unable to maintain peace. Texas Rangers still exist—and they continue to work with Texas law officers.

---

tol had been fired (which suggests there was a second shooter). What's more, the coroner testified that Cummings's skull fracture could not have occurred simply by falling to the ground (which raises the possibility that he was hit on the head before he was shot).

Unfriendly feelings

Stoudenmire was furious about Cummings's murder and wanted to punish the Mannings. Noting the growing hostility, the El Paso *Lone Star* newspaper printed that the city streets could be "deluged with blood at any moment." Concerned about the growing feud between the marshal and the wealthy Mannings, the El Paso city council convinced Stoudenmire— after three weeks of negotiating—to sign a truce (peace agreement) with the brothers. The agreement was signed on April 16, and was published, word-for-word, in the El Paso *Herald:*

> We the undersigned parties having this day settled all differences and unfriendly feelings existing between us, hereby agree that we will hereafter meet

and pass each other on friendly terms, and that bygones shall be bygones, and that we shall never allude [refer] in the future to any past animosities [ill will] that have existed between us.

The truce was short-lived. A heavy drinker, Stoudenmire often taunted and threatened the Mannings. City officials passed an ordinance making it illegal for city officers to indulge in drunkenness—a law that was clearly aimed at the town's unruly marshal. Public sentiment was against Stoudenmire as well. The *Lone Star* published the following editorial, which called on city officials to "stop dilly-dallying" and:

> to make a proper investigation, to do it with open doors, and then remove or reinstate the marshal. If he has not done his duty, or if his continuance in office is a threat to the city, he ought to be removed. Public policy dictates that, even if a man be a good peace officer, if he be obnoxious in the community, or if his continuance in office is liable to provoke serious trouble, perhaps even a riot, he ought to be replaced. Let the city act only from a high sense of duty and quit dilly-dallying.

On May 27, 1882, the city council met to dismiss Stoudenmire. When Stoudenmire appeared, he cursed and threatened them—and the meeting was called off. The following week he submitted a letter of resignation. Although he apologized for his behavior, he complained that he had been wronged by the city's politicians. In a unanimous vote (a vote in which everyone agrees), James Gillett was approved as the city marshal.

Showdown at the Manning Saloon

On September 18, 1882, Stoudenmire (who was said to be drunk) got into an argument at the Manning saloon. According to some accounts, he was looking for a fight. Others report that he entered the Manning saloon with a warrant hoping to locate a wanted criminal. The Mannings, hearing that Stoudenmire

City marshal: job description

In the Old West, the city marshal was usually appointed by the mayor and the town council. Acting as a chief-of-police, the marshal usually appointed a deputy and a number of assistant lawmen. In emergencies, the marshal was authorized to enlist the help of citizens. The marshal's authority extended only to the city limits (in theory, at least), and the town council had the power to dismiss him if they were displeased with his performance. Depending on his reputation, a city marshal in the middle of the nineteenth century earned between $50 and $250 a month.

Take a look at this!

If you like stories about lawmen in the Old West, *High Noon* (1952) is an Oscar-winning classic. In it, town marshal Will Kane (played by Gary Cooper) faces four professional killers alone—after he's been abandoned by the townspeople who claim to admire him.

had been to their saloon, assumed that he was stirring up trouble. The following day, the Mannings picked a fight with Stoudenmire.

However the fight started, it ended in gunfire. George Manning got off the first shot. The bullet ricocheted into Stoudenmire's chest, and then another shot struck him in his shirt pocket. Although the second bullet didn't wound him—since it had been stopped by the papers in his pocket—it did send him crashing through the saloon doors.

Stoudenmire, meanwhile, had managed to fire a shot that forced Manning to drop his gun. Before Stoudenmire could shoot again, Manning wrestled him into a bear hug. At that point, Manning's brother, Jim, arrived. He fired once and missed: his sawed-off revolver was missing the trigger. Jim fired a second shot using his thumb to trigger the hammer. It struck Stoudenmire in the head, killing him. Still enraged, George Manning pistol-whipped Stoudenmire's corpse until lawmen pulled him away. Tried individually for the murder of Dallas Stoudenmire, George and Jim Manning were each acquitted (found not guilty). The judge ruled that Jim had acted in defense of his "unarmed" brother. Having died a poor man, Stoudenmire was buried in a suit and coffin that were paid for by El Paso freemasons. His grave, in Columbus, has since been lost.

THE MANNING BROTHERS

Frank Manning became El Paso's marshal in April 1883. After he was dismissed for threatening a citizen, most of the Manning brothers left town. Frank turned to prospecting, and was eventually committed to a state-run institution.

Jim Manning moved from Arizona to Washington state. He married Lenor Isabelle Arzate, a woman from Juarez, Mexico. In April 1915 he died from cancer and the effects of a bullet wound he'd received earlier in life.

George Manning moved to Flagstaff, Arizona, where he continued to practice medicine. He never recovered use of the arm that had been wounded in the gunfight with Stoudenmire.

Sources for Further Reading

Collins, James L. *Lawmen of the Old West.* New York: Franklin Watts, 1990, pp. 27–35.

Metz, Leon Claire. *A Gallery of Notorious Gunmen from the American West.* New York: Berkeley Books, 1996, pp. 87–110.

Nash, Jay Robert. *The Encyclopedia of World Crime.* Wilmette, IL: Crime Books, 1990, pp. 2864–2865.

O'Neal, Bill. *Encyclopedia of Western Gunfighters.* Norman, OK: University of Oklahoma Press, 1979, pp. 78–79, 214, 302–305.

Rosa, Joseph. *The Taming of the West: Age of the Gunfighter.* New York: Smithmark, 1993, pp. 169–173.

Sifakis, Carl. *The Encyclopedia of American Crime.* New York: Facts on File, 1982, p. 691.

Old West nightlife

The Coliseum Saloon and Variety Theatre—one of the many drinking establishments owned by the Mannings—was a class establishment. It advertised a "seating capacity of 1,500, a stage 30 by 40 feet, and carpeted private boxes with elegant lace curtains."

Pancho Villa
(Doroteo Arango)

Born: June 5, 1878
Died: July 19, 1923

A gifted soldier and strategist, Pancho Villa (pronounced VEE-yah) spent a decade fighting for Mexico's freedom. But Villa was also a killer who was capable of tremendous cruelty. He was both loved and feared by his countrymen, and, by the end of his career, had few admirers north of the border.

HEAD FOR THE HILLS!

Born on June 5, 1878, Doroteo Arango was the son of a field laborer in San Juan de Río, Mexico. His parents—Augustín Arango and Micaela Arambula—died when he was very young, and the orphaned Arango took charge of protecting his siblings. As a field worker, he was forced to work long, back-breaking hours that allowed him no time for school.

When one of the owners of the estate where he worked assaulted his sister, Arango killed the man and fled to the mountains. Still just a teenager, he lived as a fugitive from the law, calling himself "Francisco Villa"—the name of an earlier outlaw. Soon, he became known as "Pancho Villa." Villa spent years in the mountains, living off the land—and robbing, looting, and raiding banks, trains, mines and more. Because he shared his spoils with the poor, he soon became popular with the people of northern Mexico—something that would serve him well later in life.

A CALL TO ARMS

In 1909, Villa joined Francisco Madero's uprising against Porfirio Díaz, who had proclaimed himself the temporary dictator of Mexico. Quickly recognized as a brave soldier, Villa helped lead Madero and his supporters to victory over Díaz in 1911. Once his enemy had been toppled, Villa continued to fight to protect Madero's government, which had come under attack.

A suspicious man by nature, Villa sometimes aroused the suspicion of others—including his commanding officer, General Victoriano Huerta. In 1912, during the rebellion of Pascual Orozco, the general condemned the thirty-four-year old revolutionary to death. When Madero discovered that his loyal soldier was to be killed, he ordered a stay of execution. With the execution stopped, Villa was sentenced to prison in Mexico City.

But not for long. Four months later, Villa escaped to El Paso, Texas, where he began to reorganize his followers. In February of 1913, Huerta had Madero killed, and took over as dictator. Villa saw this as a call to arms. Within a month, he and eight followers crossed the muddy waters of the Rio Grande at midnight—on horses they had stolen in El Paso—in order to recruit an army from Villa's native territory.

AN UNEASY ALLIANCE

Villa's army—called the *División del Norte,* or the Division of the North—was mostly made up of *peons* (poor, landless workers) who came from cattle ranches and small towns in northern Mexico. Criminals, soldiers of fortune, miners, gamblers and even some women—who were called *soladera*—joined the ranks. A rebel army, Villa's band survived as young Doroteo Arango had—by stealing, rustling, and extorting.

Revolutionary leader
Pancho Villa and
his troops in Mexico
City, 1914.

Victoriano Huerta was a harsh dictator and he was responsible for the death of Madero, who had inspired Villa to fight for a Mexico free from oppression. Villa was determined to overthrow the man who had once condemned him to die. Joining forces with Venustiano Carranza, another rebel military leader, he scored a number of victories over Huerta and gained control of northern Mexico. By the end of 1913, Villa had become the most powerful general in northern Mexico. As governor of the state of Chihuahua, he attempted to address some of the needs of the poor: his troops cleaned the streets in Chihuahua City, he built schools, gave land to peons and printed money—even though he had nothing to back it up. In the United States, President Woodrow Wilson was so impressed with Villa's potential as a candidate for the Mexican presidency that he sent his personal representative, George C. Carothers, to visit the former bandit chieftain.

In June of 1914, Villa and Carranza succeeded in deposing (removing from power) Huerta, who had become Mexico's president—even though the United States did not recognize him as such. With Huerta removed from power, Villa and Carranza entered Mexico City as allies. By December 1914, however, Villa—by then Carranza's bitter enemy—was forced to flee the city with Emiliano Zapata, a revolutionary leader who opposed Carranza. The two exiles waged a series of guerrilla attacks against the Carranza government.

A survivor's story

Jessie L. Thompson was four years old at the time of the Columbus massacre. Her grandfather, William Taylor Ritchie, owned the Commercial Hotel, one of the targets of the ambush. By the end of the raid, William Ritchie and three of his guests had been shot dead. Here's what his granddaughter recalls:

On March 9, 1916, at about 4:00 A.M. the Ritchie family was awakened by shouting and shooting in the street. Peering cautiously out of the window, as stray bullets ricocheted off the stovepipes and walls of the rooms, they could dimly see horses and hear the pounding of hooves. . . . Bandits on foot were running and shooting in every direction and smashing storefronts with the butts of their rifles. Entering the stores, they bayoneted bags of flour and unrolled bolts of cloth in the streets. They swept what had been orderly rows of merchandise on the shelves into ruined piles of trash.

—*excerpted from* American Heritage *magazine,
December 1996*

But Villa had met his match. After losing a number of battles, Villa and Zapata were forced to retreat to the mountains of the north. Then came the death-blow to Villa's military power: in April 1915, Alvaro Obregón—a general in Carranza's army—defeated Villa's troops at the Battle of Celaya. A savvy strategist, Obregón applied what he had learned from reports of the war in Europe—World War I, which changed the face of modern warfare. Instead of old-fashioned cavalry-style warfare such as Villa used—attacking his enemy on horseback—Obregón fought a modern battle—choosing a battleground and defending his ground. He directed his troops to wait for Villa—that is, after they had dug trenches, positioned barbed-wire entanglements, and posted machine guns. Three times Villa attacked, and three times his cavalry was cut down.

Pancho Villa was a much-married man. By some accounts, he had as many as twenty-nine wives—many of whom he had "married" by his own proclamation. In 1946, the Mexican legislature recognized Soledad Seanez la Viuda de Villa (later known as Soledad Seanez Holguin) as Villa's lawful wife after proving that they'd had a civil and a church wedding on May 1, 1919. Soledad outlived her husband by some seventy-three years. Villa's widow died on July 12, 1996—at the ripe old age of one hundred.

BAD BLOOD

Once again a bandit leader, the former General of the North withdrew to Chihuahua, where many people still viewed him as a Mexican Robin Hood. No longer a contender as a national leader, Villa watched as his countrymen shifted their loyalty to Carranza—whose government was officially recognized by the United States. This, along with the U.S. embargo on his munitions (supplies), infuriated Villa.

Villa—who had once made it a point to protect American lives and property—turned his anger against the people whose government he felt had betrayed him. In January of 1916, a gang of *Villistas* (followers of Villa) stopped a train from Chihuahua City. On board was a group of American mining engineers who planned to reopen a mine at Cusihuiriachic, in the state of Chihuahua. Most were executed. Although Villa protested that he was not to blame, many assumed that the massacre was intended to prove that Carranza didn't control the North.

Two months later, another slaughter ensued. On March 9, 1916, the small New Mexico border town and military camp of Columbus was visited by a band of guerrillas who rode through the streets, shooting out windows as they shouted *"Viva Villa! Viva México! Muerte a los americanos!"* ("Long live Villa! Long live Mexico! Death to the Americans!") Ambushed in their sleep, the Americans fought back with butcher knives, baseball bats and boiling water. By the end of the raid, the city had become a smoking ruin, and seventeen Americans—including nine civilians—were dead.

BLACK JACK PERSHING'S WILD GOOSE CHASE

Within days, U.S. president Woodrow Wilson had sent Brigadier-General John "Black Jack" Pershing to Mexico with strict orders: capture Villa—*dead or alive*. Pershing's Punitive Expedition—the last true cavalry action to be mounted by the U.S. army—led some ten thousand American soldiers into the mountains and deserts of Villa's native Chihuahua. Pershing's troops pushed 400 miles into Mexico, as far south as the city of Parral, where they were forced, after a battle, to retreat to bases in northern Mexico.

Eleven months after American troops crossed the Mexican border, the expedition was abandoned. Pershing's epic chase had cost U.S. taxpayers a whopping $130 million—and Villa was still at large. In fact, no U.S. soldier had even seen the fugitive *bandido!* Worse yet, the failed expedition had strained relations between the United States and Mexico, whose people resented the very presence of the U.S. military on Mexican soil. In an ironic twist of fate, Pershing's expedition had managed not to capture Villa—but to help *him* capture the imagination of the Mexican people, who viewed the infamous Pancho Villa as a hero for resisting the Americans.

MEANWHILE, BACK AT THE RANCH . . .

As long as Carranza was in office, Villa continued his attacks against the Mexican government. In 1920, however, he retired from the guerrilla life (fighting as an outlaw soldier). After Carranza died in the rebellion of Agua Prieta, his government was overthrown. In his place, the Mexican legislature had appointed Adolfo de la Huerta, a Sonoma governor. During his brief tenure, Huerta granted a pardon to all Mexicans—including Villa—who were in exile due to their political actions. What's more, Villa was given full pay as a retired military general and a 25,000-acre *hacienda* (ranch) in Chihuahua, along with fifty state-funded bodyguards. But there was one catch: Villa had to agree to lay down his arms and to refrain from participating in Mexican politics.

"Black Jack" Pershing

General "Black Jack" Pershing enjoyed a successful military career in spite of his failed Mexican expedition. He later commanded the Allied forces of World War I, and, after the war, was given the rank of General of the Armies of the United States—the highest rank ever given an American army officer.

Villa made good on his promise. For three years, the onetime guerrilla fighter led a peaceful rancher's life. But on July 19, 1923, he was involved in a final ambush. As he returned from the christening of the child of one of his men, Villa was shot to death in a hail of fire. More than three dozen bullets riddled his car, killing four of the five bodyguards with him. His assassins had been signaled—in an ironic echo of the Villistas' battle cry— by a pumpkin seed vendor who cried out *"Viva Villa!"*

Sources for Further Reading

The American West, A Cultural Encyclopedia, Volume 10. Danbury, CT: Grolier Educational Corp., 1995, pp. 1651–1652.

Carroll, Bob. *The Importance of Pancho Villa.* San Diego, CA: Lucent Books, 1996.

The Grolier Library of International Biographies. Vol. 1. Danbury, CT: Grolier Educational Corp., 1996, pp. 369–370.

"Pancho Villa Rides Again—in Tucson." *Newsweek* (August 2, 1982), p. 42.

Thompson, Jessie L. "A Visit from Pancho." *American Heritage* (December 1996), p. 28+.

Bootleggers

On January 16, 1920, the Eighteenth Amendment to the U.S. Constitution went into effect, outlawing the manufacture, transport, and sale of alcoholic beverages. Almost overnight, America went "dry." But vast numbers of Americans from all walks of life never lost their thirst for beer and spirits. No sooner had Prohibition gone into effect, when bootlegging gangs set up operations throughout the country to meet the public's demand for illegal alcohol.

Bootlegging—which involved the illegal production of beer and alcohol, smuggling spirits from outside of the country, and distributing illegal spirits—was an extremely profitable business. Rival gangs fought bitterly to retain control of—or to expand—their vast empires. On December 5, 1933, when the Eighteenth Amendment was officially withdrawn, Prohibition came to an abrupt end—and with it ended a criminal era.

In this section you'll read about some of the major bootlegging gangs and gangsters—such as "the terrible Gennas" and Hymie Weiss in Chicago, Owney Madden and Dutch Schultz in New York, and many others. Some became casualties of the gang wars, others earned prison terms—and a number of former bootleggers went on to illustrious careers in the reorganized gangs of post-Prohibition America.

Two Gun Alterie

(Louis Alterie)

Born: 1886
Died: July 18, 1935

The owner of a ranch in Colorado, Alterie was rare among bootleggers in his wild-west approach to gangster life in Chicago. Hot-tempered and often brutal, he was murdered by an unidentified killer years after retiring from his criminal rackets.

A CHICAGO RACKETEER

All that is known about Louis Alterie's background is that he was born Leland Varain in 1886. Other details about his life may—or may not—be true. He was probably born in either Denver, Colorado, or Los Angeles, California. According to some accounts, he boxed in the early 1900s, using the name of Kid Haynes. Other reports have him working on the right side of the law in Colorado, where he earned the position of lieutenant in the Denver police department.

By 1922, Alterie had settled in Chicago, Illinois, where he was arrested with the leader of the Lake Valley Gang, Terry Druggan, for robbery. They were charged with stealing $50,000 worth of jewelry from two Chicagoans. Although the victims had gotten a good look at Alterie and Druggan, neither was willing to identify the thieves.

Alterie eventually joined the mostly Irish gang of Charles Dion O'Banion (see box, page 467), which controlled the North Side of Chicago during the early years of Prohibition (when the

No more horsing around

In the spring of 1923, Alterie's friend, Nails Morton, rented a horse from a stable on the North Side of Chicago. At some point during the ride on the Lincoln Park Bridle Path, the horse threw Morton—and in the process, Morton's skull was crushed. Alterie was enraged when he found out what happened. He reportedly rented the horse that had killed Morton—and shot it dead.

Eighteenth Amendment outlawed the manufacture and sale of alcohol). Part of his duties involved fixing union elections by using violence to sway the outcome. Alterie roughed up union leaders in order to convince them to elect him and his associates to the presidency of several unions. Some of the terms were for life. In one incident, Alterie and other gangsters beat the leaders of the Theatrical and Building Janitors' Union. Following a brief election, Alterie was voted into a life term as the union's president. Alterie's union activities reportedly earned him $50,000 each month—not including the money he passed on to gang leader O'Banion.

Alterie quickly became a wealthy man. He bought real estate with his earnings, including nightclubs, restaurants, apartment buildings, and even theaters. And he purchased a ranch near Gypsum, Colorado—a three-thousand-acre piece of property that would serve him well during the Chicago gangland wars.

AN O'BANION GANGSTER

For a long time O'Banion's gang enjoyed the protection of politicians and police, who received large bribes (money gained by dishonest means) for their assistance. Judges, police officials, and politicians all lined their pockets with O'Banion's money. Even Chicago mayor William "Big Bill" Thompson was on the gangster's payroll. O'Banion expressed his thanks with more than money. He used his position to influence voters. In some cases, he guaranteed that entire wards (sections of a city) would vote for his man.

As one of O'Banion's top mobsters, Alterie took part in gang wars to control bootlegging activities during Prohibition. The O'Banion gang battled with rival gangsters from **Al Capone**'s (see entry) gang, the Druggan-Lake Valley Gang, the O'Donnell Brothers, and the **Genna brothers** (see entry). As an O'Banion gunman, Alterie reportedly killed more than twenty gangsters in numerous shootouts.

A HANDSHAKE MURDER

In 1924, O'Banion was slain in what became known as the "handshake murder." O'Banion owned a flower shop on North State Street, which served as a front (cover) for his criminal activities. When three men arrived at the shop, supposedly to pick up wreaths of flowers for a funeral, one shook hands with him, while the others shot him. The three men—who worked for Capone—left the North Sider dead in his flower shop.

Alterie was enraged, and he made no effort to hide it. When police captain John Stege had Alterie brought in for questioning, he reportedly boasted, "If those cowardly rats have any guts they'll meet me at noon at State and Madison and we'll shoot it out." In front of police officials and reporters, Alterie proposed an Old-West-style shootout at high noon at Chicago's busiest intersection. Captain Stege was not amused.

Stege was not the only one who disapproved of Alterie's grand threats. The surviving leaders of the O'Banion gang—such as **Hymie Weiss** (see entry) and **Bugs Moran** (see entry)—disapproved of the attention Alterie's threats drew to the gang. But Alterie did not let up. At O'Banion's funeral, he staged a tearful performance for reporters beside the coffin of his former boss. "I have no idea who killed Deanie [O'Banion]," he said. "But I would die smiling if only I had the chance to meet the guys who did, any time and any place they mention and I would get at least two or three of them before they got me. If I knew who killed Deanie, I'd shoot it out with the gang of killers before the sun rose in the morning and some of us, maybe all of us, would be lying on slabs in the undertaker's place."

Chicago mayor William Dever did not appreciate Alterie's flair for dramatic remarks, which had been printed in the daily newspapers. He reportedly demanded, "Are we still abiding by [following] the code of the Dark Ages?" Following Dever's instructions, Chicago police began to hound Alterie and other O'Banion gangsters. They stormed saloons and gambling houses that were run by Weiss and Moran, ending the gang's former protection from such police raids.

Lousy neighbors

Alterie has been given credit for inventing a particular type of ambush assassination. First, he rented a second-floor room that faced the street. Across the street was an address his target visited regularly—such as an apartment or business. Next, he installed heavy artillery in front of the apartment windows. From his second-story perch, Alterie simply picked off his victim when he came into sight.

Prohibition--the Eighteenth Amendment and the Volstead Act

By 1909, there were more saloons in the United States than there were schools, libraries, hospitals, theaters, parks, or churches. There was one saloon for every three hundred Americans, and the saloons were mainly concentrated in cities. (These establishments were not distributed evenly across the United States. There were more bars in Chicago than there were in the entire South, for instance.)

Medical evidence suggested that alcohol was seriously harmful. Adding to the social problem was a political one: most taverns were controlled by brewers or the liquor trust. Many in the era came to consider those two as an interest group, like the railroads, insurance companies, or other manufacturers who were more concerned with profit than with the public welfare.

In the years before World War I (1914–1918), the temperance movement (a movement that advocated refraining from consuming alcoholic beverages) had succeeded in convincing the legislatures (groups of individuals empowered to make laws) of twenty-six states to enact laws banning the manufacture and sale of alcoholic beverages. The long campaign was at first directed against saloons, and later against the production of alcoholic beverages. The movement's success was dramatically affected by the nation's preparations for war.

The need to conserve grain and the importance of maintaining some appearance of discipline and devotion to a patriotic cause added to the success of the movement. Toward the end of 1917, both houses of Congress had approved a resolution to amend (alter) the U.S. Constitution to outlaw the manufacture, transportation, or sale of alcoholic beverages. By January 1919, forty-six of the forty-eight states had ratified (formally approved) this proposal. Only Rhode Island and Connecticut had not. The amendment became effective on January 16, 1920. Meanwhile, the Volstead Act was passed to provide for the enforcement of the amendment.

The Eighteenth Amendment was officially withdrawn on December 5, 1933, when the Twenty-first Amendment was ratified, allowing the legal manufacture and sale of alcohol.

HOME ON THE RANGE

Alterie had become a hindrance to the O'Banion gang. His boasting had brought the gang's activities under public scrutiny (examination). What's more, his threats against O'Banion's killers angered the gang's leaders, who wanted to wait until the time was right to strike back at Capone's men. Weiss and Moran reportedly ordered Alterie to retire to his ranch in Colorado.

Alterie left Chicago's gangland wars in the mid-1920s, when he moved with his wife to his Colorado ranch. While he reportedly continued to control the unions he had ruled in Chicago, his former associates were killed in the gangland wars. Weiss was murdered in 1926. Seven others were slaughtered in the notorious St. Valentine's Day Massacre in 1929. Moran's power in the underworld faded. His former rival, Capone, was still living—although he was jailed for failing to pay taxes on his income.

LOOSE LIPS SINK SHIPS

In 1935, Alterie was called as a government witness in the trial of Ralph "Bottles" Capone—who, like his brother, Al, had been charged with tax evasion. At first, Alterie said nothing to help the government convict Capone. But when he was threatened with charges of perjury (lying in court, under oath), he testified against Ralph.

It was not long before Alterie was gunned down in a gangland ambush. On July 18, 1935, the former gangster was caught in a blast of machine-gun fire. His wife, who had been behind him, was unharmed. As he lay on the sidewalk mortally wounded, Alterie reportedly said to his wife, "I can't help it, Bambino [Baby], but I'm going." Alterie's murder was never solved.

What goes around comes around

Alterie eventually suffered the consequences of introducing the ambush murder to gangland Chicago. He was gunned down in front of his union offices—from the second-story window of an apartment across the street. Inside, investigators found machine guns poised at the windows facing the street. Alterie had been killed by a gunman who used the same method Alterie himself had used to eliminate enemies.

Sources for Further Reading

Nash, Jay Robert. *Bloodletters and Badmen.* New York: M. Evans: 1973, pp. 104–106.

Sifakis, Carl. *The Encyclopedia of American Crime.* New York: Facts on File, 1982, pp. 7–8.

Sifakis, Carl. *The Mafia Encyclopedia.* New York: Facts on File, 1982, pp. 17–18.

The Genna Brothers

Active: 1912-1925

The six Genna brothers were among the first gangsters in the city of Chicago to build an empire that took advantage of the prohibition of alcohol. Once key players in the bootlegging wars, the brothers faded from importance. Three met violent deaths, while the others lived out unremarkable lives.

Rough Kids

The Genna brothers—Angelo, Antonio, Jim, Mike, Pete, and Sam—were born in Marsala, Sicily. After immigrating to the United States in 1910, the Genna family settled in Chicago, Illinois. When they were still young boys, their mother died, leaving their father, a railroad worker, to care for them. The Genna boys grew up in a violent and crime-ridden environment. They ran around the neighborhood with little supervision. The area, known as Little Italy, was populated by Sicilian immigrants and plagued by criminals who readily committed bombings and murders.

When their father died, the teenaged Genna brothers looked to **Diamond Joe Esposito** (see entry) for guidance. A Sicilian immigrant himself, Esposito tutored the Gennas in the use of violence as a means for self-advancement. By 1912, three of the Genna brothers were involved in the **Black Hand Society** (see entry)—using violence and the threat of violence to force the residents of Little Italy to pay extortion fees. The other three brothers—Antonio, Jim, and Peter—carved out their own business in the Chicago underworld. Jim opened a house of prostitution, using his two brothers as pimps.

THE BOOTLEG EMPIRE

When Prohibition (when the Eighteenth Amendment outlawed the manufacture and sale of alcohol) was enacted in January 1920, scores of gangsters seized the opportunity to make money producing illegal alcohol. The Gennas realized that this moonshine (illegally distilled liquor) business would be much more profitable than their extortion and prostitution rackets. They put many fellow immigrants to work producing illegal alcohol. Soon, Little Italy became a vast moonshine operation under the direction of the Genna brothers.

At first, the Gennas entered into an agreement with the powerful criminal duo of Johnny Torrio and **Al Capone** (see entry), who controlled the South and West sides of Chicago. They sold their cheap alcohol to the Torrio-Capone gang, who then distributed the booze to saloons throughout the area. But the Gennas soon tired of settling for a small percentage of the profits. In less than one year, they claimed a section of the Near West Side of Chicago as their own. Opening their own speakeasies (drinking clubs), they gained exclusive control of the territory. Soon the Genna's booze empire posted staggering returns—which amounted to $350,000 each month.

THE TERRIBLE GENNAS

Torrio and Capone feared the Genna brothers, who became known as "the Terrible Gennas." The Genna brothers employed a gang of ruthless killers, including Sam "Smoots" Amatuna, Guiseppe "the Cavalier" Nerone, and Orazio "the Scourge" Tropea. Also on the Genna hit squad was an infamous pair of assassins: Albert Anselmi and John Scalise. Vicious gunmen, Anselmi and Scalise were known for dipping the tips of their bullets in garlic. They believed—mistakenly—that garlic-tipped bullets would cause a deadly infection in victims who did not die imme-

Cultured killers

The Genna brothers were not uncultured killers. They attended opera performances in front-row seats and ate at fine restaurants. Anthony Genna—who was known as "Tony the Gentleman" and "Tony the Aristocrat"—lived in an exclusive hotel in downtown Chicago, studied architecture, and even constructed model tenements for poor immigrants from his native Italy. The brothers were also deeply religious. Each reportedly carried a crucifix in his pocket—right next to his gun.

Demon alcohol

The Gennas produced cheap, vile-tasting, and sometimes deadly illegal booze. Their awful alcohol reportedly caused several deaths each year and was responsible for blinding dozens of other drinkers.

Final farewells

When Angelo Genna was killed by O'Banion gunmen, his brothers staged an elaborate funeral. Angelo was laid to rest in a $10,000 bronze casket. The men who carried the coffin wore tuxedos. The grave site was festooned with more than $25,000 worth of flowers. Most of the residents of Little Italy attended the solemn affair. Tony Genna's funeral was far less spectacular. Buried just two months after his brother, Angelo, "Tony the Gentlemen" was laid in an inexpensive wood coffin. No flowers adorned the grave site. And no one other than reporters and policemen attended the burial—not even his longtime girlfriend. Tony's mourners were scared off by the prospect of being gunned down by Capone's bloodthirsty hitmen. Ironically, Tony was buried a few feet from O'Banion—the man whose gang had been responsible for Angelo's death.

diately from their wounds. Anselmi and Scalise were also given credit for introducing the "handshake murder." While one gangster pretended to greet their victim with a friendly handshake, the other produced a gun. Unable to draw his own weapon, the helpless victim was then shot at close range.

When Torrio and Capone attempted to unite Chicago gangs under the same leadership, they found the Genna brothers very difficult to manage. Vicious and quick to kill, they ignored the territorial boundaries of rival gangsters. Eventually Chicago splintered into three rival factions: the Torrio-Capone Gang on the South and West sides, the Genna brothers on the Near West side, and the O'Banion mob on the city's North Side.

A BLOODY END FOR ANGELO

In 1924, Anselmi, Scalise, and another gangster named Frankie Uale (known as Yale) reportedly assassinated Charles Dion O'Banion (see box, page 467), the leader of the North Side gang. As O'Banion shook the hand of one of the gangsters, he was gunned down by the others. O'Banion's murder was committed as a favor to Capone.

Soon the Genna brothers began to expand their activities in Chicago's underworld. But the killing of O'Banion had sparked a wave of violence against the West Siders. One after another, the Genna brothers fell in gangland ambush killings. First to die was Angelo—known as "Bloody Angelo" for his murderous temperament. On May 25, 1925, he left his suite at the Belmont Hotel, on the North Side of Chicago. (While he made arrangements to purchase a new home, Angelo was living at the hotel, in the midst of O'Banion territory, with his wife, Lucille Spingola. The couple had been married only weeks earlier.)

As Angelo drove away from the hotel, he was followed by another car. Angelo drove to Ogden and Hudson streets unaware that he was being followed. Suddenly he realized a long black sedan was pursuing him. He sped up and turned a corner so fast that he lost control. Angelo's $6,000 automobile crashed into a post, trapping the gangster behind the steering wheel. Unable to reach his gun, Angelo remained in the car as the sedan approached. Inside was a squad of O'Banion gunmen: Vincent "the Schemer" Drucci, **Bugs Moran** (see entry), **Hymie Weiss** (see entry), and driver Frank Gusenberg. Leaning out the open windows, the gangsters pummeled Angelo's car with gunfire. His body blasted apart by the hail of bullets, Angelo died in his car.

On the take

The Genna organization did not rely on violence alone. They paid Chicago policemen to ensure that the law would not interfere in their illegal activities. The Gennas reportedly paid $200,000 *each month* to the many policemen who were on their payroll. In 1925, when the Genna's office manager made a formal confession, the former employee stated that four hundred uniformed officers and five police captains accepted Genna payments.

A SECOND GENNA FUNERAL

Mike Genna swore revenge for his brother's death. He enlisted the family's top killers, Anselmi and Scalise, to help carry out the hit. But—without Mike's knowledge—Anselmi and Scalise had joined forces with Capone. On June 13, 1925—a little less than a month after Angelo's death—Mike Genna, Anselmi, and Scalise went on a mission to find and destroy Angelo's killers. Or so Mike thought. The outing was actually a setup to allow the traitorous duo to ambush Mike.

But the hitmen never had a chance to strike. A squad car containing four Chicago police officers spotted the gangsters. Convinced that the car contained weapons, they pursued the vehicle. The gangsters' car spun out of control and crashed. Mike, Anselmi, and Scalise fled with their shotguns in hand.

A shootout followed—one policeman was killed and two others were wounded. Anselmi and Scalise fled, leaving Mike alone to battle with officer William Sweeney. After shooting Mike in the leg, Sweeney took the gangster into custody. The wound turned out to be fatal: Mike, who had been struck in an artery, bled to death before doctors could operate.

The bootleg generation

Support for the Eighteenth Amendment remained strong in the years immediately following its ratification. As late as 1928, those calling for its repeal (withdrawal) were a minority. The Volstead Act (1919) seemed to have the intended effect. But there was no doubt that large numbers of people still wanted to drink.

With overall production severely restricted, prices rose dramatically. The situation ushered in an era of lawlessness greater than any in recent memory. Enforcement became increasingly difficult and, much to the disgust of the supporters of Prohibition, unenthusiastic.

Many were prepared to risk arrest to take advantage of the opportunities that bootlegging (the illegal manufacture and sale of alcohol) presented. Closing the legal channels of supply had given thousands the incentive to become bootleggers and operators of clubs that dis-pensed liquor that became known as "speakeasies." Liquor dealers in Canada, the Caribbean, and Europe provided a ready and uninterrupted source of alcoholic beverages. Local stills (distilleries) often operated day and night to produce cheap and illegal booze.

Toward the end of the Prohibition era, much of the organized effort to transport, sell, and distribute alcohol had fallen under the control of criminal gangs. Many of the gangs reflected a particular ethnic origin and possessed enough wealth and political influence to link cities and entire regions within the networks they had created. As the gangsters gained in power and prominence, and as the perception of public corruption became more pronounced, Americans became more unhappy with the government's efforts to enforce the law. Meanwhile, rival gangs waged war with one another. It has been estimated that more than one thousand people died in the Chicago bootleg wars alone.

THE DEATH OF TONY GENNA

Afraid for his life, Tony Genna refused to leave his suite at the Congress Hotel. There, Guiseppe Nerone contacted him. He informed Tony that Capone was responsible for his brother's death—and he suggested that they meet to decide on a plan to get rid of the South Side mobster. Tony agreed. He was aware that Anselmi and Scalise had joined forces with Capone. But he was not aware that Nerone, too, had deserted him.

On July 8, 1925, Tony met Nerone at Curtis and Grand Avenue. As the two men shook hands, two other men appeared from a doorway and shot at Tony. Struck several times in the back, he was taken to County Hospital, where he died days later. The two shooters were said to be Anselmi and Scalise.

OLIVE OIL AND CHEESE: THE END OF THE GENNA DYNASTY

One after another, Genna supporters were ambushed by Capone hit squads. Henry Spingola—Angelo's politician father-in-law, who had taken over the Genna family's business affairs—was gunned down by Tropea, who had deserted the Genna gang for Capone's camp. Vito Bascone was murdered as he begged, on his knees, for his life. Ecola Baldelli was cut to pieces by his assassins, who threw his remains in a garbage dump. Tony Finalli and Felipe Gnolfo also died at the hands of Capone's killers.

The remaining Genna brothers fled Chicago. After years in hiding, Jim, Peter, and Sam Genna returned to their former home in Illinois—but not to their former rackets. No longer a part of the Chicago underworld, they operated an importing firm that dealt in olive oil and cheese. The three surviving Genna brothers lived the remainder of their lives in obscurity.

Sources for Further Reading

Nash, Jay Robert. *The Encyclopedia of World Crime.* Wilmette, IL: Crime Books, 1990, pp. 1291–1294.

Sifakis, Carl. *The Encyclopedia of American Crime.* New York: Facts on File, 1982, pp. 278–279.

Machine Gun Kelly
(George Barnes)

Born: 1897
Died: 1954

A likable—although none-too bright—small-time crook, Kelly became a legend in his own time. With the prodding of his image-conscious wife, Kathryn, the non-violent bootlegger was molded into a gun-toting gangster known as "Machine Gun" Kelly. Guilty of only one major crime, a kidnapping, he was eventually captured and imprisoned for life.

A BOOTLEGGER NAMED BARNES

Born and raised in an impoverished Tennessee community, George Barnes received little schooling. A petty (small-time) crook as a teenager, he sometimes produced illegal alcohol. When Prohibition (when the Eighteenth Amendment outlawed the manufacture and sale of alcohol) went into effect, he began a full-time bootlegging business (the illegal manufacture and sale of alcohol). Operating in Memphis, Tennessee, he provided wealthy individuals and clubs with liquor that had been smuggled from Canada—where U.S. Prohibition laws did not apply. Barnes changed his name to Kelly during his bootlegging days.

Criminal gangs fought viciously to retain control of their territories and to expand their profitable bootlegging operations. When Memphis gangsters learned that Kelly was moving in on their territories by selling to speakeasies (drinking clubs), they threatened his life. A non-violent man, he promptly abandoned his bootlegging activities and moved out of state. Kelly eventually landed in New Mexico, where he attempted to

Nobody said he was smart

When Kelly's in-laws were arrested for kidnapping, the gangster sent a threatening letter to Charles Urschel, the man he had kidnapped. He urged Urschel to drop the case, writing:

Ignorant Charles—

If the Shannons are convicted look out, and God help you for He is the only one that will be able to do you any good. In the event of my arrest I've already formed an outfit to take care of and destroy you and yours the same as if I was there. I am spending your money to have you and your family killed—nice, eh? You are bucking people who have cash—planes, bombs, and unlimited connections both here and abroad. . . . Now, sap [sucker]—it is up to you, if the Shannons are convicted you can get you another rich wife in Hell because that will be the only place you can use one. Adios [goodbye], smart one,
Your worst enemy,
Geo. R. Kelly
I will put my prints below so you can't say some crank wrote this.

Kelly sent the damaging letter—with his fingerprints—to Urschel. While his in-laws eventually received light sentences for their role in the kidnapping, Kelly was sentenced to life in prison.

resume his bootlegging business. But in 1927, as he made a liquor delivery, he was arrested. Convicted of violating the Volstead Act (drawn up in 1919 to enforce the prohibition of alcohol), he was sentenced to three months' imprisonment. After he was released from the New Mexico State Prison, Kelly moved to Fort Worth, Texas, where he picked up where he had left off— delivering bootleg liquor.

A SHARE-CROPPER'S DAUGHTER

While Kelly worked as a rum runner (transportation of illegal alcohol) between Fort Worth and Oklahoma City, Oklahoma, he met a beautiful young woman named Kathryn Thorne. Born in Saltilo, Mississippi, in 1904, Thorne was the daughter of a poor farm laborer. She later changed her birth name, Cleo, to Kathryn—because she thought the name was more sophisticated. At the age of fifteen she married a local boy, with whom she had a daughter. She soon divorced her husband and moved with her child to Coleman, Texas, where she joined her mother (who had left her father).

Coleman was the home of her mother's family, many of whom were crooks who ran illegal stills and brothels. Thorne's mother eventually married a man named R. G. "Boss" Shannon, who ran a ranch near Paradise, Texas. Shannon added to his income by turning his ranch into a criminal hideout where he housed and fed wanted criminals—in exchange for a fee.

When her daughter was two years old, Thorne left the girl with her mother and moved to Fort Worth, Texas. Working at a hotel as a manicurist, she met many men who were passing through town on business. She sometimes worked as a prostitute, and was arrested two times for soliciting. At the age of twenty, she met and married a bootlegger named Charlie Thorne. Three years later, he was found shot to death, with a note that said, "I can't live with her, or without her, hence I am departing this life." Many people objected that the language in the suicide note did not sound like something Charlie would have written. In fact, it sounded much like his wife, Kathryn, who liked to used formal expressions (such as "hence") to make herself look more sophisticated. Although Thorne had reportedly told a gas station attendant that she was going to kill her husband days before he was found, the death was ruled a suicide. She inherited what remained of the bootlegger's estate.

A THORN IN HIS SIDE

Kelly met Thorne in 1927. At the time, she is said to have been helping bank robbers by making trips to out-of-town banks and reporting back with information about the bank's layout and procedures. Thorne immediately began to mold Kelly into something that he was not: a hardened, big-time crook. She gave him a submachine gun and bragged to others that he was a daring and fearless bank robber. She reportedly made him practice shooting for hours at her family's Texas ranch. Eventually Kelly became a good shot—and even boasted that he could shoot walnuts off a fence at twenty-five yards and *never even damage the fence*. In reality, the easy-going gangster disliked weapons and avoided violence. It's quite possible that "Machine Gun" Kelly never killed anyone.

Still involved in the bootlegging business, Kelly was arrested in 1930, when he drove onto an Oklahoma Indian reservation with a truckload of liquor. He was given a brief sentence at Leavenworth prison, where he was well-liked by inmates as well as guards. A model prisoner, he landed a job in the prison's records office. Thorne pressed him to befriend some of the more important prisoners, who would be able to help him when he was released from jail. Taking her advice, he became acquainted with bank robbers Thomas Holden and Francis Keating. Using his position in the records office, he secured fake passes. The two gangsters used the passes and borrowed clothes to walk out of prison before their terms were up.

The FBI story

J. Edgar Hoover, the director of the FBI, claimed that Kelly acted as a coward when he was captured by FBI agents. Kelly supposedly cowered with his hands in the air, begging, "Don't shoot, G-men [government men]—don't shoot." But Hoover, who fought to bolster the reputation of the FBI (and its director) was sometimes guilty of creating an "FBI version" of event, which placed the agency in a favorable light.

When Kelly was released the following year, he married Thorne. Working with a few other gangsters, the couple staged a number of bank robberies from 1931 to 1933. Using Thorne to case the businesses (study the layout of a business to plan a crime), the Kelly gang raided banks in Mississippi, Washington, and Texas. Although most of the holdups went off without violence, a job in Wilmer, Texas, left one guard dead. Thorne bragged that Kelly was the shooter—but it was probably one of the other gang members.

A BUMBLING KIDNAPPER

Kelly's bank robberies did not bring in enough cash to satisfy Thorne, who enjoyed expensive things. They decided to follow the lead of other criminals, who had collected large sums of money by kidnapping wealthy individuals. On July 22, 1933, Kelly and a middle-aged burglar named Albert Bates entered the mansion of Oklahoma City oil millionaire Charles F. Urschel. To their surprise, they found two couples playing cards. Since the kidnappers had neglected to find out what Urschel looked like, they did not know which of the two men was their intended victim. And none of the four card players volunteered to identify him.

Kelly and Bates took both men outside, where Thorne was waiting in a getaway car. As they drove out of town, Kelly col-

Machine Gun Kelly (center), flanked by heavily armed police and justice officers, is escorted to the airport on October 2, 1933. Headed for Oklahoma City, Oklahoma, Kelly would stand trial for the kidnapping of Charles Urschel.

lected each man's wallet. Once he identified Urschel, he dropped the second man, Walter R. Jarrett, on an empty country road. Urschel was taken, blindfolded, to Thorne's family ranch in Texas, where he was held in a one-room shack.

In spite of a few miscalculations, the kidnappers eventually collected the $200,000 ransom they demanded. A friend of the millionaire, E. E. Kirkpatrick, gave Kelly a briefcase full of money on Linwood Avenue in Kansas City, Missouri—in exchange for a promise that Urschel would be returned home within twelve hours.

WAITING FOR THE POLICE

Thorne reportedly wanted to kill Urschel to make sure that he did not identify his kidnappers, while Kelly and Bates insist-

The Alcatraz rebellion and escape

During Kelly's imprisonment at Alcatraz federal prison, located on an island in San Francisco Bay, California, a number of other inmates staged a rebellion. On May 2, 1945, prisoners started a riot and, securing weapons, fought a gun battle with prison guards in an effort to shoot their way out. For the first time in the history of "the Rock," as Alcatraz was known, inmates were able to obtain firearms during their attempt to escape.

The escape plan began to take shape when three inmates, Bernie Coy, Joseph "Dutch" Cretzer, and Miran "Buddy" Thompson, joined forces in Alcatraz. Coy had designed and built a bar spreader and had figured out a way to gain access to the prison armory (where weapons were kept). The three ringleaders and three other inmates staged an uprising in a cellblock and took nine guards as hostages. U.S. marines were ordered to the island prison to reinforce the officers.

On the second day of the riot, occasional fighting continued between the guards and convicts. The inmate leaders attempted to negotiate a deal with prison officials, but this was refused with a demand for total surrender. On the third day of the uprising, when it became apparent that the inmates would not succeed, Thompson ordered Cretzer to kill the hostages since they were the only ones who could identify Thompson as being involved in the escape attempt.

Against Coy's orders not to kill any hostages, Cretzer shot all nine. During the last stages of the battle, Coy and Cretzer were killed. Secure in the belief that his own involvement in the uprising would remain unknown, Thompson returned to his cell. Surprisingly, only one of the guards shot by Cretzer had actually been killed. Thompson was later convicted of murder and sentenced to death. On December 3, 1948, he became the first person put to death in the California gas chamber.

ed on letting him live. They drove him, blindfolded, to the edge of Oklahoma City, where they left him with $10 for taxi fare. Once the millionaire arrived home safely, Federal Bureau of Investigation (FBI) agents questioned him about the incident. He had an excellent memory, and provided agents with information that eventually led them to the Shannon ranch in Texas.

When FBI agents arrived at the ranch, they found Thorne's mother and her husband, "Boss" Shannon, as well as her son, Armand (Thorne's stepbrother). The three were charged in the kidnapping. Kelly and Thorne, who had driven to Chicago, remained at large. But after Bates was picked up in Denver, Colorado, the couple moved south, to Memphis, Tennessee, near where Kelly had grown up. There, residents recognized him and informed the police where he was hiding.

On September 26, 1933, three Memphis police detectives—Detective Sergeant W. J. Raney and Detectives A. O. Clark and Floyd Wiebenga—captured Kelly and Thorne in the small bungalow they were using as a hideout. After dropping the automatic gun he held, Kelly reportedly told officers, "I've been waiting all night for you."

FATE OF THE KIDNAPPERS

Tried and convicted of kidnapping, Kelly, Bates, and Thorne were sentenced to life in prison. Thorne's family, who had hidden the kidnappers, received lighter sentences. Kelly was jailed at Alcatraz Prison, California, until 1954, when he was transferred to Leavenworth Prison in Kansas. He died from a heart attack later that year. Thorne remained in the Cincinnati Workhouse for Women until she was paroled in 1958.

Sources for Further Reading

Bruns, Roger. *The Bandit Kings From Jesse James to Pretty Boy Floyd.* New York: Crown, 1995, p. 168.

Nash, Jay Robert. *The Encyclopedia of World Crime.* Wilmette, IL: Crime Books, 1990, pp. 1782–1787.

Sifakis, Carl. *The Encyclopedia of American Crime.* New York: Facts on File, 1982, p. 390.

Owney Madden

Born: 1892
Died: 1965

Transplanted as a child to a tough New York neighborhood, Madden soon earned the nickname, "the Killer," because of his reputation as a cold-blooded killer. While violence came back to haunt many of his hot-headed associates, Madden lived quietly—and very comfortably—until the age of seventy-three.

A YOUTHFUL GOPHER

Madden was born in Liverpool, England, in 1892. After his father died, the eleven-year-old moved to New York City to live with his aunt in a poor and violent neighborhood known as Hell's Kitchen. Shortly after his arrival he became a member of a violent street gang called the Gophers. As a young gangster, Madden earned a reputation as a violent and dangerous criminal. He committed muggings—using various weapons, including brass knuckles, a sling shot, and a lead pipe wrapped in newspaper—and fought with members of a rival gang, the Hudson Dusters.

Madden soon rose to the gang's top ranks. As the leader of the Gophers, he planned robberies, killings, beatings and other crimes for which he reportedly collected $200 per day. Barely out of his teens, Madden became involved in an "insurance business." For a fee, he provided bomb insurance to local shopkeepers. Dozens of merchants paid the sum, well aware that if they refused, the gangsters would strike back by bombing their busi-

Madden committed his first murder when he was seventeen years old. Police believed that he had killed his victim not for revenge or retaliation—but to celebrate being promoted to the top position in the notorious New York gang, the Gophers. The police were not able to prove the case against Madden.

nesses. By the time Madden was twenty-three years old, he was believed to have been responsible for five murders. During his time as a Gopher, he was arrested forty-four times—but he was never jailed. Witnesses to the violent gangster's criminal activities rarely stepped forward to accuse him.

LEFT FOR DEAD

In 1910, a clerk named William Henshaw attempted to date one of Madden's many girlfriends. Madden followed Henshaw onto a Manhattan trolley car, where he shot the man in front of passengers. Before jumping from the trolley, he rang the conductor's bell. Henshaw lived long enough to identify Madden as the shooter. Two weeks later, police arrested the gangster in a daring rooftop chase. Charged with murder, Madden was set free after witnesses refused to testify against him.

Madden announced that he planned to become the boss of the New York underworld. He strengthened his position by hiring a number of deadly gunmen, including Eddie Egan, Chick Hyland, Tanner Smith, and Bill Tammany. But as his power grew, so did the resentment of rival gangs.

On the evening of November 6, 1912, eleven members of the Hudson Dusters followed Madden to the Arbor Dance Hall on Fifty-Second Street. A shootout followed. By the end of the gunfight, Madden had been hit several times. The Dusters left him for dead.

In spite of his several wounds, Madden survived. In the hospital, he refused to identify his attackers. Following the gangster's code of silence, he reportedly told police that the matter was nobody's business but his own. By the time he was released from the hospital, six of Madden's assailants had been gunned down by members of the Gopher gang.

THE MURDER OF PATSY DOYLE

Madden's troubles were not over: a gangster named Patsy Doyle was moving in on his territory. By some accounts, he wanted to take over the leadership of the Gophers. By other accounts, he was angry because Madden had begun seeing his girlfriend, Freda Horner.

Whatever his reasons, Doyle set out to ruin Madden—and Madden knew it. On November 28, 1914, Madden arranged for Doyle to appear at a bar at Eighth Avenue and 41st Street in Manhattan. He shot Doyle three times. Sentenced to twenty years in prison for the murder, Madden was paroled after nine years.

BOOTLEGGING AND BOXING

Released from Sing Sing prison in 1923, Madden discovered that the Manhattan underworld had been reorganized around the bootlegging business (the illegal manufacture and sale of alcohol, which took place when the Eighteenth Amendment was ratified in 1920). In Prohibition-era New York, the remains of the Gopher gang had been absorbed into other rumrunning mobs (gangs that transported illegal alcohol). After a brief period working as a strikebreaker, Madden formed a new gang and staked his claim in the illegal liquor industry. Together with **Dutch Schultz** (see entry), an established bootlegger who headed the numbers racket (gambling) in Harlem, he fought for control of bootlegging activity in New York. Throughout the 1920s, Madden and Schultz battled with other powerful bootleggers, such as Vincent "Mad Dog" Coll, **Legs Diamond** (see entry), and Waxey Gordon.

As Prohibition came to an end, Madden sought out other opportunities. In the 1930s, he became involved in fixing boxing matches. Working with "Broadway" Bill Duffy and "Big

A social butterfly

When a reporter asked Madden how he spent his days, the gangster began to keep a journal to record his activities. The journal revealed a busy social calendar:

Thursday—Went to a dance in the afternoon. Went to a dance at night and then to a cabaret. Took some girls home. Went to a restaurant and stayed there until seven o'clock Friday morning.

Friday—Spent the day with Freda Horner. Looked at some fancy pigeons. Met some friends in a saloon early in the evening and stayed with them until five o'clock in the morning.

Saturday—Slept all day. Went to a dance in the Bronx [an area in New York City] ate in the afternoon, and out to dance on Park Avenue at night.

Sunday—Slept until three o'clock. Went to a dance in the afternoon and to another in the same place at night. After that I went to a cabaret and stayed there almost all night.

Prizefighter Primo
Carnera, champion of
fixed boxing matches.

Frenchy" DeMange, he promoted Italian boxer Primo Carnera.
A large but untalented fighter, Carnera became heavyweight
champion by winning a series of fixed matches. Carnera held
the heavyweight title until June 14, 1934—when he was severely beaten by one of Madden's associates. The boxer earned nothing from his brief career: Madden reportedly claimed all of
Carnera's earnings, which amounted to $1 million.

The difficult task of enforcing Prohibition

The discovery off the New Jersey coast of a flexible pipeline used to connect the bootleggers' boats to the bootleggers' fleets of trucks said a lot about their boldness and inventiveness. It also revealed the extent to which local and national Prohibition agents had become powerless to do anything meaningful about it.

In 1921, Mabel Walker Willebrandt was appointed an assistant to the U.S. attorney general. Assigned the task of overseeing the Justice Department's efforts to enforce the newly passed Volstead Act (drawn up in 1919 to enforce the prohibition of alcohol), she discovered that few colleagues took this responsibility seriously. Worse still was the fact that her authority did not extend to local police officers who were largely responsible for enforcing the law.

In New York, where a state Prohibition law had been in effect since 1921, sixty-nine hundred arrests had been made during one three-year period—but only twenty convictions had been obtained. Willebrandt's attention soon focused upon the U.S. attorneys in federal districts around the country, many of whom she criticized for their lack of commitment. But corruption ran wild among the Prohibition agents. Willebrandt gave up in 1928.

In 1930, attorney general William N. Mitchell appeared before the Senate Judiciary Committee to criticize Congress for not providing President Herbert Hoover (1874–1964) with the funds he needed to improve the government's ability to enforce Prohibition. Admitting that efforts to enforce the law were losing their power, he called for more prisons and longer prison terms for offenders. Many marveled at the attorney general's persistence. He would have done better, they felt, if he had heeded the advice of his former assistant, Willebrandt, when she concluded that what federal enforcement required was not more men, money, and ammunition but greater respect for its own purpose and responsibility.

THE HIGH LIFE IN HOT SPRINGS

Madden found himself in jail again in 1932, when he was arrested for parole violation. Released after a short time in prison, he was followed by policemen who arrested him frequently on minor charges. Tired of his constant troubles with the law, Madden retired from the New York underworld. A millionaire several times over, he moved to Hot Springs, Arkansas, a favorite vacation spot among mobsters.

Working for mobster **Meyer Lansky** (see entry), Madden opened several casinos in Hot Springs. As one of the leaders of the area's thriving gambling activity, he enjoyed the protection of local police. After marrying the daughter of the postmaster, he became a citizen in 1943. When Madden died in 1965, his estate was estimated to be worth $3 million.

Sources for Further Reading

Nash, Jay Robert. *The Encyclopedia of World Crime.* Wilmette, IL: Crime Books, 1990, pp. 2072–2073.

Sifakis, Carl. *The Encyclopedia of American Crime.* New York: Facts on File, 1982, pp. 459–460.

Sifakis, Carl. *The Mafia Encyclopedia.* New York: Facts on File, 1982, pp. 204–206.

Bugs Moran
(George Moran)

Born: 1893
Died: 1957

Moran was the target of one of the most brutal episodes in gangland Chicago: the St. Valentine's Day Massacre. But, by a stroke of luck, he was not among those slain. Formerly the commander of the North Side's bootlegging empire, Moran died poor, and in prison—for a minor robbery.

A POLISH CROOK IN AN IRISH GANG

A native of rural Minnesota, George Moran moved to Chicago, Illinois, as a teenager. There he found himself in a mostly Irish area on the city's North Side, where Irish street gangs controlled the neighborhood. Pretending to be of Irish rather than Polish descent, Moran joined one of the area's all-Irish gangs.

During his teens, Moran—now known to some as "Bugs"—befriended Charles Dion O'Banion (see box, page 467). The young Irish crook taught Moran what he needed to know about burglary and safe cracking. By the time he reached his seventeenth birthday, Moran was an experienced criminal. Before he was twenty-one, Moran had reportedly committed at least twenty-six known robberies. He was arrested for the first time in 1910, although he was not convicted. During the next several years, he managed to stay out of prison in spite of frequent arrests. But on May 24, 1918, Moran was convicted of armed robbery and sentenced to serve time at Joliet State Prison in Illinois.

ENEMIES OF CAPONE

On February 1, 1923, Moran was released on parole (the release of a prisoner before his time has expired). Fresh out of state prison, he headed back to his former gang. Under O'Banion's direction, the gang had begun to thrive during Prohibition (when the Eighteenth Amendment outlawed the manufacture and sale of alcohol). By bribing policemen and politicians, the gang operated breweries and distilleries without fear of being shut down. The gang also controlled the illegal distribution of alcohol. Soon O'Banion's gang became the most powerful bootlegging gang on the city's North Side.

At the time, bootlegging activities on the South Side of Chicago were controlled by Johnny Torrio and **Al Capone** (see entry). O'Banion's gang often raided the South Siders' territory. Moran and others from O'Banion's gang hijacked the trucks carrying Torrio and Capone's beer and liquor shipments. They beat up bar owners and bartenders who bought their liquor from the rival mobsters to force them to purchase O'Banion's product.

On November 10, 1924, O'Banion was murdered by gunmen from the Torrio-Capone organization. While **Hymie Weiss** (see entry) took over the leadership of the North Side gang, Moran was next in the line of command. First on their agenda—revenge for O'Banion's murder.

TORRIO RETIRES

Torrio, who was responsible for ordering O'Banion's murder, was at the top of the North Side gangsters' hit list. On January 24, 1925, Moran, Weiss, Peter Gusenberg, and Vincent "the Schemer" Drucci ambushed the South Sider as he returned home with his wife. As the couple stepped out of their limousine at their address on South Clyde Avenue, Weiss and Drucci fired at them with shotguns. Wounded, Torrio fell to the ground.

Moran rushed across the street to finish him off. He placed a revolver at Torrio's head and pulled the trigger. But the gun did not fire. By then police were approaching. Moran and the other North Siders fled, leaving Torrio and his wife behind. Although he'd been struck four times, Torrio survived.

Shaken by his brush with death, Torrio retired, leaving Capone in charge of the South Side's thriving bootleg business. The twenty-five-year-old gangster was more than happy to take Torrio's place. In fact, some people suspect that it was Capone who had an informer provide the North Siders with information about Torrio's whereabouts.

AT WAR WITH THE GENNAS

Throughout the rest of the year, the North Side gang continued to kill off rival gangsters who had been involved in O'Banion's murder. Among their targets were the **Genna brothers** (see entry), a rival bootlegging gang that had ties with Capone. The Gennas had reportedly provided two of the three hitmen who had ambushed O'Banion: Albert Anselmi and John Scalise.

The North Siders struck on May 25, 1925. Angelo Genna—who was known as "Bloody Angelo" because of his murderous disposition—was their target. Moran, Weiss, and other members of the O'Banion gang hunted Genna in a car chase through the city's North Side. They opened fire on Genna's car with shotguns and submachine guns. Genna crashed into a post and was trapped behind the steering wheel. The North Siders pulled up beside him in a black sedan and fired three blasts of shotgun fire—Angelo was dead.

For more than a year, the Gennas waged war against the North Side gangsters. On June 13, 1925, they struck on Michigan Avenue, a busy street in the center of town. A car filled with Genna gunmen ambushed Moran and Drucci just as they were about to walk into a building. Caught in a hail of machine-gun and revolver fire, both North Siders were wounded—but not killed. As police rushed to site of the shootout, the hit men fled. Questioned by police, Moran and Drucci refused to name the shooters—even though they knew exactly who they were. Most gangsters followed a code of silence that prevented them from naming their attackers.

FIREWORKS AT THE HAWTHORNE INN

The North and South Side gangs continued to wage war. They engaged in shootouts in full daylight, on streets crowded with innocent bystanders. The violence peaked on September 20, 1926. Ten cars filled with North Side gangsters drove to Capone's headquarters in Cicero, on the southwest side of Chicago. They struck at noon. As the gunmen drove by, they fired thousands of shots into the Hawthorne Inn. They focused on the coffee shop on the first floor—where Capone and his bodyguard were trapped. Caught in the shootout, both gangsters and innocent bystanders shielded themselves against the flurry of shotgun, submachine gun, and revolver fire. Amazingly, no one was killed, and only a few were wounded.

Capone had seen his attackers. Louis Barko, one of the Capone gang's most respected hitmen, soon received clear instructions from his boss: destroy the North Side gangsters. Barko attacked twice—and twice he failed. But on October 11, 1926, Weiss became a casualty of the gang wars when he was shot to death as he crossed the street near Holy Name Cathedral. As luck would have it, Moran was not with him.

MORAN TAKES CHARGE

Moran, who had been second in command, took charge of the North Side gang. He met several times with Capone to arrange a peace treaty—which both gangsters were quick to ignore. While Moran agreed not to interfere with Capone's operations on the South Side, Capone promised not to operate north of the "Dividing Line" (Madison Street, in the heart of downtown Chicago).

Moran made a point of demonstrating that he was not afraid of Capone. After he was married, he drove around town with his wife in an open car. Popular with newspaper reporters, he informed them where he would be—and when. And he took every opportunity to badmouth Capone. He told reporters that the North Side gang were gentlemen bootleggers who simply addressed a public need. Capone, on the other hand, was a "lowlife" whose underworld activities were not confined to bootlegging. Unlike the North Side gang, Capone's mob dealt in prostitution.

A BLOODY VALENTINE

In 1929, Capone began to disregard the "Dividing Line" completely. After the South Sider's gunmen began to invade the North Side, Moran joined forces with mobster Joseph Aiello. An enemy of Capone, Aiello posted a $50,000 reward for the murder of the man known as "Scarface."

A pauper's funeral

Most of Moran's associates were buried in expensive funerals—with lavish floral arrangements, extravagant coffins, solemn processions, costly headstones, and large crowds of mourners. But Moran—who was once a millionaire—was given a pauper's burial when he died in Leavenworth prison in 1957. He was laid in a plain wooden casket and buried in a potter's field—a public burial place for paupers, unknown persons, and criminals.

With two of Moran's top gunmen—Frank and Peter Gusenberg—Aiello murdered Capone's good friend, Pasquilino Lolordo. As the three men sat drinking wine in Lolordo's living room, they shot their unsuspecting victim to death. Capone knew who the killers were—and that the murder had taken place with Moran's blessing. He swore revenge.

First he killed Aiello as he attempted to skip town. Capone reportedly committed the murder himself. Next, he targeted Moran. Using a mobster from Detroit, Michigan, he arranged an ambush at Moran's headquarters at 2122 North Clark Street. The Detroit mobster approached Moran, claiming to have a shipment of hijacked booze for sale. Moran took the bait—and arranged to take delivery at the gang's headquarters on the morning of February 14, 1929—Valentine's Day. But there was no liquor shipment. Instead, a hit squad appeared at Moran's headquarters, killing several of the North Side mobsters.

Moran was not among them. Arriving late to the meeting, he noticed three men dressed as policemen and two others in street clothes entering the gang's garage headquarters. He assumed that a police raid was taking place. Accompanied by his bodyguards, Willie Marks and Ted Newberry, he waited at a nearby

Bugs Moran, right, and his attorney, George Bieber, in court on April 22, 1938. Moran was charged with forging $200,000 worth of money orders.

coffee shop. Soon the garage was ablaze with machine-gun fire, which killed six gangsters and one innocent bystander.

DOWN AND OUT

Moran no longer made light of his rival, Capone. He reportedly checked into a hospital, where his bodyguards maintained a constant watch. Once friendly with reporters, he refused to answer their questions. Asked about the massacre, he replied, "I don't know. I don't know anything about it." But newsmen continued to question him until he finally blurted, "Only Capone kills like that!"

The shootout—which became known as the St. Valentine's Day Massacre—marked the end of Moran's career as a gangland boss. Although he continued to maintain political control of the North Side area for the next few years, he never recovered from Capone's vicious attack. By 1940, Moran exercised no power in the Chicago underworld.

His fortune spent, Moran survived by pulling small burglaries. With most of his associates dead—and deserted by his wife—he no longer had ties to Chicago. He moved to Ohio after World War II (1939–1945), where he joined forces with a couple of petty crooks, Albert Fouts and Virgil Summers. In 1946, the three men robbed an Ohio bank messenger of $10,000. Moran was soon arrested by Federal Bureau of Investigation (FBI) agents and sentenced to prison. Released after ten years he was again arrested—for a bank robbery he had committed before he was sent to prison. Moran died of cancer in Leavenworth penitentiary. He was sixty-four.

Sources for Further Reading

Nash, Jay Robert. *The Encyclopedia of World Crime*. Wilmette, IL: Crime Books, 1990, pp. 2213–2215.

Sifakis, Carl. *The Encyclopedia of American Crime*. New York: Facts on File, 1982, pp.498–499.

Dutch Schultz
(Arthur Flegenheimer)

Born: August 6, 1902
Died: October 23, 1935

Unreliable and governed by self-interest, Dutch Schultz was nevertheless included on the board of the national crime syndicate organized by Lucky Luciano and other crime bosses of the era. When his hot temper threatened to attract too much heat to the organization, his associates ordered him killed—with little regret.

YOUNG FLEGENHEIMER

Arthur Flegenheimer—who later took the name Dutch Schultz—was born in New York City, on August 6, 1902. His parents were Emma and Herman Flegenheimer. Raised in the Bronx, Schultz dropped out of school after the fourth grade. He soon joined the Bergen Gang—a gang of juvenile thieves and pickpockets.

When Schultz was just fourteen, his father deserted the family. Emma Flegenheimer supported herself and her teenaged son by taking in laundry for pay. A warm and kind woman, she tried to convince Schultz to return to school. But he looked for his education on the streets of New York.

Armed with burglars' tools, Schultz committed numerous burglaries and holdups as a teenager. He worked for a while as a printer—simply to provide a front for the more profitable business of theft. In 1919, at the age of seventeen, he was arrested for burglary and sentenced to a fifteen-month prison term.

The expensive apartment building in New York's exclusive 5th Avenue neighborhood where Dutch Schultz lived.

BACK ON THE STREET

Time behind bars did little to reform Schultz. After serving out the entire sentence, he returned to his earlier occupation. With the earnings from several robberies, he purchased a bar in the Bronx and began to assemble a fierce gang of thugs. Among the men in his gang were Abe Landau, Julie Martin, Joey Rao,

Arthur Flegenheimer was afraid that his given name was too long to appear in newspaper headlines. Following his release from prison, he changed his name to Dutch Schultz—the name of an earlier gang leader. Shortly before the turn of the century, the original Dutch Schultz headed a band of Bronx gangsters known as the Frog Hollow Gang.

Lulu Rosencranz, and brothers George and Abe Weinberg.

Schultz continued to open illegal bars during Prohibition (when the Eighteenth Amendment outlawed the manufacture and sale of alcohol), which he stocked with liquor that had been smuggled from Canada and Europe and whiskey that had been stolen from rival bootleggers. He also served home-made beer, which was considered to be among the area's worst. Schultz's gang soon expanded its operations to include areas of Manhattan. But the new territories did not come easily. A number of rival gangsters were killed in the process.

NUMBERS GAMES AND ONE-ARMED BANDITS

Always on the lookout for new opportunities to make money, Schultz did not limit his activities to the illegal liquor business. In Harlem and other areas of New York, African American gangsters controlled an illegal gambling operation known as the numbers racket—also called the policy racket. Most of Schultz's associates ignored the numbers racket, believing that it was a nickel-and-dime operation that provided little earning potential. But Schultz knew otherwise.

Schultz and his gunmen threatened Stephanie St. Clair, who presided over the numbers racket in Harlem. The cold-blooded mobster gave her a choice: allow him to take over her business, or face Schultz's death squad. St. Clair turned over her operations—and other Harlem numbers leaders followed. The numbers racket was a nickel-and-dime business. But most of Harlem's population wagered nickels and dimes on a daily basis. The business yielded millions of dollars, and Schultz amassed a private fortune.

By the 1930s, Schultz became involved in another money-making enterprise: the slot machine business. Working with **Frank Costello** (see entry) and Joey Rao, he and his gang flooded New York City with gambling machines known as one-armed bandits—some of which were equipped with step-ladders so that children could play. Again, it was a nickel-and-dime business. And again, it reaped millions for Schultz and his colleagues.

DIAMOND LOSES HIS SPARKLE

Schultz hired a number of notorious mobsters to protect his many illegal operations. Gunman Vincent Coll and a number of young gangsters delivered Shultz's beer and liquor to various New York speakeasies (bars that sold illegal alcohol). **Legs Diamond** (see entry), whose gang controlled a portion of Manhattan's bootlegging empire, lent Schultz added muscle.

But Schultz's alliance with Diamond did not last long. By 1930, their partnership had dissolved. Schultz's beer shipments often disappeared: his delivery trucks were hijacked by rival gangsters. When he learned that Diamond was responsible for the thefts, he declared war on Diamond's gang. The gang war claimed several casualties from both sides.

Because he lived through numerous attempts on his life, Diamond became known as the "clay pigeon of the underworld." For a while it looked like he was impossible to kill. But on December 19, 1931, Diamond was killed when two Schultz gunmen tracked him to upstate New York, burst into his hotel room, and repeatedly shot him. Schultz later told reporters that the dead gangster "was just another punk with his hands in my pockets."

THE COLL WAR

Schultz also found himself in a gang war with Vincent Coll and his brother Peter. The Colls' followers beat up bartenders and bar owners who purchased liquor from Schultz. Using violence, they forced their victims to stop buying Schultz's booze—and to purchase their own product instead. Coll also began to take over Schultz's profitable numbers racket.

Although Coll's gang was small, his mobsters killed a number of Schultz's top men. In June 1931, Schultz and his bodyguard, Danny Iamascia, saw two men loitering on a street in Manhattan. They thought they were about to be ambushed by

"You're dead"

Schultz's lawyer, Dixie Davis, was quoted as saying, "You can insult Arthur's [Schultz's] girl, spit in his face, push him around—and he'll laugh. But don't steal a dollar from his accounts. If you do, you're dead."

the Coll brothers. A shootout followed, in which Iamascia was fatally wounded. Schultz fled, and one of the men followed him. The man wrestled him to the ground in an alley and identified himself.

The man was not, as Schultz feared, one of the Coll brothers. He was New York Police Detective Steve DiRosa. The other man was Detective Julius Salke. The two detectives had been following the bootleg czar to find out more about his operations. Booked on charges of attempted murder, carrying a concealed weapon, and resisting arrest, Schultz was not detained long. Thanks to one of the many judges who received bribes from the gangster, he was released on bail and the charges were eventually dropped.

A FATAL PHONE BOOTH

The incident fueled Schultz's grudge against Coll. The following year, one of his men followed Coll to find out more about his daily habits so that he would be more vulnerable to attack. Schultz learned that Coll often used a phone booth inside a drugstore on West 23rd Street. From the drugstore phone booth, Coll made many "business" calls—including ransom calls to **Owney Madden** (see entry), whose partner had been kidnapped.

On February 8, 1932, Coll was making a phone call to Madden when one of Schultz's men saw him. The man contacted Abe and George Weinberg, two gunmen for the Schultz gang. The Weinberg brothers arrived at the drugstore with two other men as backup. First, one man escorted the store clerk and two customers to a room in the back. Then another opened fire on Coll, who was still in the phone booth. Several rounds of bullets shattered the glass booth, killing Schultz's rival.

TRIED FOR TAX FRAUD

Schultz's next battle was with the government. Having earned millions of dollars from his various illegal rackets, the mobster had neglected to pay taxes on his income. After the state of New York estimated that Shultz owed millions of dollars in back taxes, he was charged with income tax evasion.

Many of Schultz's peers had received long jail terms on similar charges. But, with the help of his lawyer, Dixie Davis, Schultz managed to beat the charges. Davis managed to have the trial moved out of New York City—where his client was a high-profile gangster—to a town in rural upstate New York. Schultz also employed a public relations firm that helped to improve his public image in the local community. The agency made sure that everyone in town knew about Schultz's many donations to local charities and other favorable activities. By the time Schultz was tried for tax evasion, Schultz had many supporters. The jury found him not guilty.

WEINBERG'S REWARD

When Schultz returned to New York City, he found that many of his rackets had been taken over by Vito Genovese and Lucky Luciano. What's more, his former aide, Bo Weinberg, had helped Schultz's rivals gain control of his operations. Schultz reacted by moving his headquarters from the Bronx, in New York, to Newark, New Jersey. Schultz also gave the order to kill Weinberg. Some said that Schultz personally shot Weinberg in the head. Others claimed Schultz's former aid was encased in cement and dropped into the Hudson River—while he was still breathing. Evidence suggests that **Bugsy Siegel** (see entry) carried out the hit—by stabbing Weinberg repeatedly.

A SYNDICATE MAN

Schultz returned to New York at a time when crime leaders were busy organizing the underworld into a national crime syndicate. He was offered a position on the syndicate's board of directors—not because he was a loyal associate, but because he would pose a powerful threat as an enemy. Concerned only with his own rackets, Schultz had no regard for the interests of the other board members. The other board members considered "the Dutchman" to be unreliable. And they wanted to gain control of his bootlegging and numbers rackets. In short, they wanted him dead.

Charles Workman, the man who killed Dutch Schultz.

No more slots

By 1935, Schultz saw his vast slot machine empire destroyed. Backed by New York mayor Fiorello La Guardia (1882–1947), New York district attorney Thomas E. Dewey launched an attack on the state's slot machine business. Hundreds of Schultz's one-armed bandits were demolished by sledgehammers and dumped in the East River. Mayor LaGuardia took advantage of every opportunity to have himself photographed as he swung a sledgehammer down on one of the gambling machines—as a symbol of his stance against crime and corruption.

Schultz's partners, Frank Costello and Phillip "Dandy Phil" Kastel, relocated their slot machine business to New Orleans, Louisiana. But Schultz, who remained on the East Coast, arrived at another solution. He planned to have Dewey murdered.

Schultz informed the crime syndicate board of his plan to kill Dewey. Concerned about the attention such a murder would attract, the board members refused to approve the killing. But Schultz planned to make the hit with or without the board's approval. He reportedly left the board meeting shouting that he would do the killing himself—within forty-eight hours.

The board members had little time to react. They voted to have Schultz killed and appointed Albert Anastasia to take care of the matter. Anastasia had recently been put in charge of Murder, Inc. A hit squad for the newly formed national syndicate, Murder, Inc. was charged with taking care of gangsters who challenged syndicate decisions. Anastasia promised that Schultz would not live to see the next day.

THE DUTCHMAN'S DEMISE

On the evening of October 23, 1935, Schultz and three associates—his accountant Otto "Abbadabba" Berman and two bodyguards, Abe Landau and Lulu Rosencranz—met in the back room of Schultz's favorite hangout, the Palace Chophouse in Newark, New Jersey. Shortly after Schultz left the table for the men's room, three men arrived at the restaurant: Emmanuel "Mendy" Weiss, Charles "the Bug" Workman, and another man, known only as "Piggy." First, one of the gunmen charged into the men's room, where he shot a man to ensure that the gunmen would not be attacked from behind. Schultz was next to be shot. Then, the gunman fired at the men who were seated at the table.

When the gunmen fled, all of the victims were still breathing. Berman, Landau, Rosencranz, and Schultz were all taken to Newark City Hospital, where each one died. Shot in the back

Last words

Police Sergeant L. Conlon questioned Schultz in the hospital to try to find out who shot him. Many gangsters refused to identify their attackers because they followed a code of silence. Schultz was anything but silent—although he never identified his assailant. The dying gangster uttered nonsense that was impossible to understand. Conlon recorded Schultz's ramblings.

Shortly before Schultz died, the policeman asked him again to identify his shooter. The gangster responded:

I don't know. I didn't even get a look. I don't know who could have done it. Anybody. Kindly take my shoes off . . .

No, there's a handcuff on them. The baron says these things. I know what I am doing here with my collection of papers. It isn't worth a nickel to two guys like you or me, but to a collector it is worth a fortune. It is priceless. I am going to turn it over to. . . . Turn your back to me please. Henry, I am so sick now. The police are getting many complaints. Look out! I want that G-note. Look out for Jimmy Valentine for he is an old pal of mine. Come on, come one, Jim. Okay, okay, I am all through. Can't do another thing.

Look out mama. Look out for her. You can't beat him. Police, mama, Helen, mother, please, take me out. I will settle the indictment. Shut up! You got a big mouth! Please help me up, Henry. Max, come over here! French-Canadian bean soup. I want to pay. Let them leave me alone!

After a two-hour silence, Schultz died.

and in the side, Schultz lived the longest. When he was asked who his killer was, his garbled responses made no sense. He died two days later, without ever naming his assassins. Although Schultz never identified him, Charles Workman was convicted of the murder and sentenced to life in prison. He was paroled from the New Jersey State Prison after twenty years.

Sources for Further Reading

Nash, Jay Robert. *The Encyclopedia of World Crime.* Wilmette, IL: Crime Books, 1990, pp. 2699–2705.

Sifakis, Carl. *The Encyclopedia of American Crime.* New York: Facts on File, 1982, pp. 642–643.

Roger Touhy

Born: 1898
Died: December 17, 1959

*Roger "Terrible" Touhy was reportedly one of the few men who could force **Al Capone** (see entry) to blink in a confrontation. Framed for a crime he did not commit, he spent years in jail before he was finally paroled—only to be gunned down by someone who apparently held an old grudge.*

FROM ALTAR BOY TO OIL MAN

The son of a policeman, Touhy was born in Chicago, Illinois, in 1898. When he was ten years old, a kitchen stove exploded, killing his mother. Touhy moved with his father, two sisters, and five brothers from Chicago to the suburb of Downer's Grove, Illinois. There, he and his seven siblings had a respectable upbringing. The young Touhy served as an altar boy at the neighborhood Catholic church and was a student at St. Joseph's grade school, where he graduated from in 1911. Many of his friends went on to become police officers.

As a teenager, Touhy worked as a Western Union messenger. He eventually became a telegraph operator and managed a small Western Union office. After being fired in 1915 for participating in union activities, he moved to Colorado, where he worked as a telegraph operator for the Denver & Rio Grande Railroad.

Touhy enlisted in the United States Navy during World War I (1914–1918). In 1918, he spent the year teaching Morse code to Navy officers at Harvard University. (Morse code is a system of dots and dashes used to communicate by telegraph.) After he was discharged from the military, he again headed West. In Oklahoma, where oil was being drilled from the land, he worked in a number of towns as an oil rigger and engineer. He became involved in the profitable business of buying and selling oil leases. By the time he returned to Chicago in 1922, he had saved $25,000.

A BETTER BREW

Back in Chicago, Touhy married and started a trucking firm with his brother, Tommy, in the early 1920s. The business started off slowly. But when the Touhy brothers began to load their trucks with illegal alcohol (when the Eighteenth Amendment was enacted in 1920, it outlawed the manufacture and sale of alcohol), their business began to boom. The Touhys earned a fortune by distributing illegal beer and liquor. Soon they controlled most of the bootlegging activities in the northwestern section of Cook County in Chicago, including the suburb of Des Plaines. Using cash payoffs and fringe benefits—such as free beer—he made sure that local politicians and police officials did not interfere with his operations.

Much of the alcohol sold during Prohibition was of very poor quality. But Touhy, who had hired a leading chemist to establish a beer brewery, sold top-notch beer and liquor. Together with his partner, Matt Kolb, he manufactured what was widely regarded as the best beer in the Midwest during the Prohibition era. Profiting from his reputation as a quality producer, Touhy charged top dollar for his product. But not everyone was happy to pay a large fee for Touhy's special brew.

TERRIBLE TOUHY

Chicago mobster Al Capone was among Touhy's clients. In one notorious incident, he purchased eight hundred barrels of beer—and then attempted to pressure Touhy into lowering his price. He claimed he would not pay the full price—$37.50 for each barrel—because some of the barrels leaked. But Touhy stood his ground and Capone paid the full amount he owed. Touhy is reportedly the only gangster to have forced Capone to back away from a conflict.

But in reality, Touhy was not the fearsome man he was reputed to be. The newspapers referred to him as Roger "The Terrible" Touhy—but reports of his terror were mostly made up. The leader of what was actually a very small gang, he deliberately created a public image as a gunslinging gangster. When rival gangsters visited his headquarters in the Arch, a road house in Schiller Park, he reportedly relied on police and other associates to help him create the appearance of a large and powerful gang. He borrowed machine guns and other weapons, with which he lined the walls of his headquarters. Policemen, friends, and other locals posed as trigger-happy gangsters who were eager to follow his orders. The ploy is said to have scared away a number of would-be challengers to his bootlegging territory.

A FALL GUY

Because of Touhy's fierce reputation, few gangsters were willing to confront him. But Capone's mobsters were determined to take over Touhy's share of the Chicago bootlegging market. The mobsters reportedly used another method to force Touhy out of power: they set him up—and stood by as he was arrested for crimes he did not commit.

A taxing murder

The former bootlegger's murder was reportedly ordered by Murray "the Camel" Humphreys, a Capone mobster who had been threatened by Touhy years earlier. Six months after Touhy was killed, Humphreys purchased four hundred shares of First National Life Insurance Company stock from Jake Factor—the man Touhy had been wrongly convicted of kidnapping. He bought the stock at a price of $20 a share. Eight months later, he sold the stock back to Factor—for $125 a share. The Internal Revenue Service (IRS) decided to take a look at Humphreys's $42,000 profit. The IRS declared that the money was clearly a payment for services that had been performed. (It was not the business of the IRS to determine what those services were.) Humphreys therefore owed full income taxes on $42,000 he received from Factor. It's quite possible that the government collected taxes on money that had been paid for an execution.

Blood runs down the steps of the home of Touhy's sister where Touhy was shot down.

In 1933, Federal Bureau of Investigation (FBI) agent Melvin Purvis arrested Touhy and charged him with kidnapping William A. Hamm Jr., a millionaire brewer from St. Paul, Minnesota. Although the FBI claimed to have a strong case against him, Touhy—and gang members who had been arrested with him—were found not guilty. Members of the Barker-Karpis gang (see entry on **Ma Barker**) were later accused of the kidnapping. (Alvin "Creepy" Karpis had ties to the Capone gang.) Although it is not clear whether Capone's gang was involved in this incident, there was little doubt that they were the masterminds of a second frame-up.

Later in 1933, Touhy was again charged with kidnapping. This time the "victim" was Jake "The Barber" Factor, a con man who was known to be linked with the Capone mob. Although it was commonly rumored that the kidnapping had been staged by Factor and Capone gangsters, Touhy was taken to court. Although his first trial resulted in a hung jury, he was convicted in a second trial. (A hung jury cannot agree on a verdict.) Sentenced to ninety-nine years in Joliet penitentiary in Illinois, Touhy left the courtroom shouting that he had been framed.

Melvin Purvis, FBI

When Touhy was arrested for the kidnapping of Jake "the Barber" Factor, Melvin Purvis, a special agent in the FBI, boasted that the case had been solved because of outstanding detective work. He said, "This case holds a particular interest for me because it represents a triumph of deductive work. We assumed from the start, with no material evidence, that the Touhy gang was responsible for the crime."

But that was exactly the problem. There *was* no material evidence, because Touhy had been framed for the crime by rival mobsters who wanted to take over his bootlegging territory. The case against Touhy and the three others who were charged in the kidnapping relied on testimony that was later discovered to have been false.

FBI agent Purvis later captured the notorious **John Dillinger** (see entry) and other wanted fugitives. But the Touhy incident remained an embarrassment for him throughout his career. In 1960, just months after Touhy was gunned down, Purvis, who had retired from the FBI, committed suicide.

FREE AT LAST

At first, Touhy was a model prisoner. For years he tried to prove that he had been wrongly accused. He saw his fortune dwindle as high-priced lawyers tried to win an appeal for the former bootlegger. On October 9, 1942, after almost ten years in prison, Touhy joined six other convicts in a prison break. With him were Basil "the Owl" Banghart, Edward Darlak, St. Clair McInerney, Martlick Nelson, Eugene O'Connor, and Edward Stewart. Using a homemade rope ladder, they climbed up a prison wall to a guard's tower. From there they escaped to the outside.

The escaped convicts were soon placed on the FBI's "Most Wanted List." In December 1942, FBI agents tracked them to a boarding house in Chicago. A shootout followed. Two of the escapees died in the gunfire. The others were taken into custody. Touhy found himself back in prison—with one hundred and ninety-nine years added to his sentence.

But Touhy continued to fight his conviction. Supported by a number of reporters who believed that he had not been responsible for the kidnapping, he won another hearing in the 1950s. Touhy's lawyers argued his case in federal court, before Judge John P. Barnes. At the end of the thirty-six-day inquiry, Barnes declared that the kidnapping had been a hoax. Factor, he said, had cooperated in his "disappearance." On November 25, 1959—after close to twenty-five years behind bars—Touhy was released from prison.

The former bootlegger's fortune was gone and he was in poor health. He moved in with his sister in Chicago. On the night of December 16, 1959, as he returned to his sister's home, Touhy was gunned down by shotgun fire. Although the bullets nearly cut his body in two, he did not die right away. Before dying he reportedly said, "I've been expecting it. The bastards never forget!"

Sources for Further Reading

Nash, Jay Robert. *The Encyclopedia of World Crime*. Wilmette, IL: Crime Books, 1990, pp. 2976–2978.

Sifakis, Carl. *The Encyclopedia of American Crime*. New York: Facts on File, 1982, pp. 717–719.

Sifakis, Carl. *The Mafia Encyclopedia*. New York: Facts on File, 1982, pp. 323–325.

Hymie Weiss
(Earl Weiss)

Born: 1898
Died: October 11, 1926

As a member of Charles Dion O'Banion's North Side gang, Earl "Hymie" Weiss was involved in the longstanding territorial disputes between Chicago's North and South Siders. Weiss was killed by the familiar mob method of ambush from a second-story apartment.

THE PERFUME BURGLAR

When Polish-born Earl Wajciechowski moved to the United States with his family as a boy, he took the name of Earl "Hymie" Weiss. He was still just a boy when he was arrested, in 1908, for robbing a pharmacy. Weiss spilled perfume on his clothing during the robbery. When reporters wrote about the incident, they referred to the ten-year-old criminal as the "Perfume Burglar."

By the time Weiss was a teenager, he had become a skilled car thief and burglar. Labor unions hired him to provide muscle in union disputes—and to carry out executions when necessary. An accomplished safecracker, he found his way into the gang of O'Banion—a former alter boy who, like Weiss, was a devout (religious) Catholic who regularly attended Holy Name Cathedral. Operating out of the North Side of Chicago, O'Banion's gang concentrated on jewel thefts and various other safecracking jobs.

With valuable political connections in the North Side wards, O'Banion enjoyed some degree of protection from police

Weiss, like many other criminals of his time, was a devout church-going Catholic. The son of Polish Catholic parents, he regularly attended mass. And he reportedly never left home without a rosary and crucifix in his pocket.

and prosecution. In one case, both Weiss and O'Banion were arrested for burglarizing the Parkway Tea Room. Although their fingerprints had been found on the Tea Room's safe, both gangsters were acquitted (found not guilty). The jury had been bribed.

AN O'BANION LIEUTENANT

When Prohibition (when the Eighteenth Amendment outlawed the manufacture and sale of alcohol) went into effect, O'Banion's gang moved into the profitable bootlegging business (the illegal manufacture and sale of alcohol). Joining forces with a number of other mobsters, such as Vincent "Schemer" Drucci, Frank and Peter Gusenberg, and **Bugs Moran** (see entry), they took control of the North Side's thriving bootlegging business. Acting as O'Banion's second-in-command, Weiss convinced saloon owners to purchase the gang's liquor. Thoughtful about planning for the future, Weiss employed bribery freely. Police gave him credit for building his boss's business into a successful large-scale operation. At the height of its success, the O'Banion gang supplied bootleg booze to hundreds of establishments near the lakefront in Chicago's 42nd and 43rd Wards (political districts of a city).

As major players in the city's bootlegging business, O'Banion's gang became involved with territorial disputes with Al Capone's rival organization. Gang warfare was unavoidable. On November 10, 1924, Capone's hitmen gunned down O'Banion at the gangster's flower shop. (O'Banion operated the flower shop, a legal business, as a "front," or cover, for other illegal activities.)

Although Weiss was enraged by the killing, he prevented the gang from striking back at Capone's gang—for a while. The newly appointed gang chief was rumored to have promised O'Banion's widow that he would refrain from violence until after the funeral. Among the mourners who attended O'Banion's burial was Capone, who defiantly watched the ceremony with six of his bodyguards.

In less than two months, violence erupted. On January 12, 1925, Weiss—together with O'Banion gangsters, Drucci and Moran—attempted to ambush Capone. After following Capone's

Charles Dion O'Banion (1891-1924)

In the early 1920s, the illegal rackets on the North Side of Chicago were dominated by an Irish immigrant named O'Banion. On the surface he was a pleasant man who loved to sing the old songs of his homeland, and he spent most days working in his florist's shop on North State Street. He was also a major bootlegger and drug trafficker who was considered "Chicago's arch-criminal" by the Chicago police.

Informed insiders claimed that O'Banion—who always carried three guns concealed in special pockets made by his tailor—arranged for the deaths of at least twenty-five of his enemies. It was O'Banion who began the custom of sending large floral arrangements for the public funerals of slain mobsters. He made most of these funeral wreaths himself.

O'Banion started out as a member of a North Side juvenile street gang. His earliest adult crimes were burglary and safecracking. Because of a leg wound from an early gunfight, O'Banion walked with a pronounced limp. By the time Prohibition (when the Eighteenth Amendment outlawed the manufacture and sale of alcohol) went into effect in 1920, O'Banion's gang—an ethnic mix of Irish, German, and Jewish hoodlums—was well placed to benefit from the newly profitable racket of bootlegging whiskey.

At first, O'Banion and his major rival **Al Capone** (see entry) maintained an uneasy coexistence. But in the summer of 1924, O'Banion's henchmen began hijacking Capone's liquor trucks. They also shot up several speakeasies (bars that sold illegal alcohol during Prohibition) in Capone's South Side territory, wounding some of Capone's men. Capone would have his revenge: at noon on November 10, 1924, three gunmen entered O'Banion's shop and shot him to death. The fact that his usually reliable bodyguards were in the back room at the time raised suspicions that they had been paid to stay out of the way. No one was ever charged with O'Banion's murder.

limousine to State and 55th streets, they drove by while shooting at the parked vehicle. Although twenty-six shots had ripped into the car, only the chauffeur, Sylvester Barton, was wounded. Two bodyguards escaped without injury, as did their boss, who had stepped into a nearby restaurant moments before the shooting began. To protect himself from further attacks, Capone later ordered the construction of an expensive armored car.

Weiss continued to launch attacks against Capone. Just over one week after the restaurant shooting, Drucci and Moran wounded Capone's longtime associate, Johnny Torrio, near his

The first Chicago gangland funeral

In 1920, James Colosimo was the reputed "kingpin" of the Chicago underworld. After arriving in Chicago, Illinois, from Italy in 1895, "Big Jim" started a lucrative loan-shark operation on the South Side. By the late 1910s, Colosimo also dominated prostitution and gambling in Chicago from his headquarters at Colosimo's Cafe on South Wabash Avenue, one of the most popular nightspots in the city. There, gangsters freely mingled with figures from high society.

In 1915, Colosimo brought in his relative, Johnny Torrio, from New York City to help manage his growing operations. Five years later, Torrio arranged for another New Yorker, Al "Scarface" Capone, to join the organization.

With the beginning of Prohibition in January 1920, Colosimo began a sizable bootlegging enterprise. But his role in Chicago's bootlegging skirmishes was short-lived. Colosimo was fatally shot in the lobby of Colosimo's Cafe on the afternoon of May 11, 1920. Some claim that Frank Uale (known as Yale), a former associate, performed the killing in an attempt to "muscle in" on Colosimo's rackets. Others are certain that Capone and Torrio commissioned (ordered) the killing—although both had proof that they were elsewhere at the time. Colosimo's slaying is generally considered to be the first gangland "hit" during the 1920s.

Colosimo was the first mobster to be given a lavish public funeral. His "send-off" at the Holy Name Catholic Cathedral cost $20,000. It was also the first burial for which gangster and florist Charles O'Banion provided the extravagant floral arrangements that became standard displays at mob funerals.

South Side home. On June 13, Angelo Genna—a member of the Capone-friendly **Genna brothers** (see entry) organization—was murdered by Weiss's men.

ALL-OUT WAR

On September 20, 1926, a large contingent of Weiss's men ambushed Capone at the Hawthorne Inn—the Capone gang's headquarters on the West Side of Chicago. Eleven cars full of gunmen drove slowly by as they fired pistols, machine guns, and shotguns into the lobby of the hotel. According to reports, more than one thousand bullets ripped into the building. Capone—who had been thrown to the floor by a bodyguard—again escaped without injury.

Soon the tables turned. The day after the Hawthorne Inn shooting, Capone associates rented a room in a building across the street from Holy Name Cathedral and the O'Banion gang's headquarters at the State Street flower shop. Capone's hitmen settled into the second-floor room and waited for their victim to appear. On October 11, 1926, Weiss appeared with attorney William W. O'Brien and his bodyguards, Benny Jacobs, Paddy Murray, and Sam Peller. Capone's killers fired at them as they crossed State Street, wounding O'Brien, Jacobs, and Peller. Weiss and Murphy were shot dead. When questioned after the slaying, Capone expressed false regret: "That was butchery. Hymie was a good kid. He could have got out long ago and taken his and been alive today."

Take a look at this!

Bugsy Malone (1976) is an offbeat musical spoof of 1930s mobster movies with an all-child cast. The plot loosely concerns a gangland war between sarsaparilla (root beer) bootlegger Fat Sam and an upstart named Dandy Dan, who raids Sam's speakeasies with "splurge guns" that shoot whipped cream. A young Jodie Foster plays a gangster moll (girl-friend).

Sources for Further Reading

Nash, Jay Robert. *The Encyclopedia of World Crime.* Wilmette, IL: Crime Books, 1990, pp. 3119–3120.

Sifakis, Carl. *The Encyclopedia of American Crime.* New York: Facts on File, 1982, pp. 752–753.

Pirates

In 1837, an American named Charles Ellms wrote, "In the mind of the mariner, there is a superstitious horror connected with the name of Pirate; and there are few subjects that interest and excite the curiosity of mankind more than the desperate exploits, foul doings, and diabolical careers in human form. . . ."

Mutinies, stolen cargoes, and battles fought in the high seas. Buried treasure and sunken ships. Cruel and unusual punishments and the pirate code of conduct. There's plenty here to "interest and excite the curiosity"—and then some. In this section you'll read about the desperate exploits and foul doings of a handful of pirates who terrorized ports in the American colonies and elsewhere. Included are Blackbeard—who burned tapers in his beard to create a fiendish appearance; Charles Gibbs and Joseph Baker—mutineers who paid for their crimes on the gallows; and Anne Bonny—one of very few women pirates about whom anything is known.

Joseph Baker

Born: ?
Died: May 9, 1800

A ruthless mutineer, Joseph Baker was duped by the captain of the ship he intended to claim. Returned to the port he departed from, he was hanged in a public execution.

MUTINY ON THE *ELIZA*

Born in Canada, Baker was a pirate and murderer who sometimes worked as a merchant seaman out of the American colonies. On his last voyage he signed onto a merchant ship named *Eliza*. With Captain William Wheland at the helm, the vessel left the harbor in Philadelphia, Pennsylvania, for the warm waters of the Caribbean.

Baker did not intend to help *Eliza* reach its final destination in the Caribbean. Before departing on the voyage, he had recruited two other sailors—Joseph Berrouse and Peter LaCroix—to join him in a mutiny (open rebellion against authority). The three men waited until the ship was far from land and out of range of the assistance of other vessels. The mutineers struck at night—as one seaman watched over the ship while most of the crew slept. Surprised by the attack, the first mate (the crew member next in command to the captain) struggled with Baker and his accomplices. They threw him overboard.

The pirate code of conduct

Although pirates rejected the rules of governments, most followed a democratic organization on board ship and in port. Many pirates were required to swear to observe the rules before setting sail on a voyage. The code was printed in *Captain Johnson's General History of the Robberies and Murders of the Most Notorious Pirates*. Published in 1724, the code lists some of the rules that provided order in the sea rovers' existence. The rules included:

- Everyone may vote on all important decisions.

- Anyone keeping a secret or attempting to desert will be marooned. He may take only a flask of gunpowder, a bottle of water, a gun and some shot [ammunition].

- Anyone found stealing from another member of crew will have his ears and nose slit open, and be set ashore.

- Anyone being lazy or failing to clean his weapons will lose his share of booty.

- No one may leave the crew until each man has made one thousand pounds [British currency] worth of booty.

Having heard signs of a struggle, Captain Wheland went above deck to investigate and was wounded by the mutineers. Baker could not afford to kill Wheland: he had failed to plan a safe route to a port where the mutineers could sell the ship's cargo. Baker needed to Wheland to help him find his way in the high seas.

THE TABLES TURN

Baker informed the captain that, if he helped the mutineers sail to safety, his life would be spared. But Wheland knew that Baker had no intention of keeping his word. He bought time by promising to help the pirates reach the Spanish Main—a haven for sea robbers comprised of parts of Central and South America owned by Spain. When two of the mutineers were below deck, he shut the only entrance that led to the hold—and locked them in. Baker stood at the captain's wheel. When he saw Wheland approaching with an ax in his hand, he fled.

Wheland ordered Baker to climb to the top of the ship's main mast—and to tie himself in place with rope. For two weeks, Baker remained tied to his perch, while Wheland steered the ship toward a safe port. The captain occasionally sent the pirate something to eat and drink by using a rope as a pulley, and he lashed himself to the steering wheel to make sure that he did not accidentally fall asleep and allow the ship to veer off course.

After fourteen days of little sleep and rough seas, Wheland arrived at St. Kitts (an island in the West Indies). There he deliv-

Piracy on the Spanish Main

Shortly after Christopher Columbus sailed to the Americas in 1492, Spain laid claim to a territory known as the Spanish Main—parts of the Central and South American mainlands from Mexico to Peru. The New World territory contained vast riches—including silver mines in Ecuador and Peru and native treasures of the Aztecs and Incas. Having seized the area, the Spaniards plundered the Spanish Main. They loaded ships with jewels, gold, silver, and artifacts, and transported their booty to their native country. The solid gold jewelry of the Aztec natives was crushed and melted down in order to save room on the treasure ships.

The area became a pirate haven. As they made their way from the Caribbean Sea to the Atlantic Ocean, the Spanish galleons (a type of sailing vessel) were looted by privateers—sea robbers who had government approval to plunder enemy ships. Many of the privateers on the Spanish Main were French and English. Most attacks took place early in the return voyage. Waiting in ambush off the North American coast, privateers surprised their victims as they headed north from the Caribbean.

In 1603, King James I (1566–1625) of England attempted to put a stop to privateering in the Caribbean, when he withdrew all letters of marque—a government license that gave privateers authority to pillage (rob) the vessels of rival governments. Then, in 1630, Spain signed a treaty with France and England allowing them to colonize some of the territories in what had been the Spanish Main. By the end of the century, the Spaniards had lost much of their lands and influence in the Caribbean. As Spain's presence in the area declined, so did privateering.

But the Spanish Main soon became the center of renewed pirate campaigns. In 1713, the Treaty of Utrecht put an end to the War of the Spanish Succession among Spain, Britain, and France. Suddenly unemployed, many former sailors turned to piracy. Pirate ports flourished in the Caribbean and on mainland America. The area known as the Spanish Main—which now included the West Indies, the Gulf of Mexico, and the Caribbean (including the various Caribbean islands)—entered a golden age of piracy.

---

ered Baker, Berrouse, and LaCroix to U.S. Navy officers, who shipped the mutineers back to the port from which they had departed. The prisoners were held on board a war ship, the *Ganges.*

On April 21, 1800, the mutineers' trial began. All three were tried for piracy and murder before the circuit court in Philadelphia, Pennsylvania. The charges of piracy and murder

Piracy and profit-sharing

Pirates lived by articles of agreement that determined how the loot was divided. Historians have found evidence that the standard agreement allotted two shares of the loot to the pirate captain, one and a half shares to the quartermaster, and one share to regular seamen. Pirates who were seriously injured in battle received additional shares.

were punishable by death. Five days later, all three mutineers were found guilty. Each was sentenced to be executed. On May 9, 1800, the pirates were hanged, in plain sight of a large crowd of onlookers who attended the execution.

Sources for Further Reading

Broad, William. "Archaeologists Revise Portrait of Buccaneers As Monsters." *The New York Times* (March 4, 1997), pp. C1, C9.

Nash, Jay Robert. *The Encyclopedia of World Crime.* Wilmette, IL: Crime Books, 1990, pp. 216–217.

Platt, Richard. *Pirate.* New York: Alfred A. Knopf, 1994, pp. 20–21.

Ross, Stewart. *Fact or Fiction: Pirates.* Surrey, British Columbia: Copper Beech Books, 1995, pp. 10–11.

Smith, Simon. "Piracy in Early British America." *History Today* (May 1996), pp. 29–37.

Blackbeard
(Edward Teach)

Born: c. 1680
Died: November 22, 1718
AKA: Edward Tach, Tash, Tatch,
Thatch, Drummond

Blackbeard was a legend in his own time. Born in England, he plundered (robbed) ships traveling to and from the American colonies—as well as vessels in the Caribbean. Although his reign of terror lasted only two years, he became one of the best-known sea robbers in all of history.

FROM PRIVATEER TO PIRATE

Edward Teach was probably born somewhere near Bristol, England. Little is known of his early life—except that he went to sea as a young man. As a privateer (legalized pirate) during the War of the Spanish Succession (1701–1713), he plundered ships in the West Indies. When the war ended in 1713, he turned to piracy, like many other former privateers.

By 1716, Teach was serving under the command of Benjamin Thornigold, a pirate captain. On Thornigold's ship, he sailed from the pirate colony of New Providence in the West Indies to the American mainland. The pirates captured a number of ships, whose cargo ranged from flour and wine to silk and gold bullion (gold still in raw or unrefined form). In 1717, after the pirate crew attacked a large merchant ship headed for the French island of Martinique, Teach took over as the captured vessel's captain. Equipping the boat as a warship, he added some forty guns and renamed it the *Queen Anne's Revenge.*

Read all about it!

The year after Teach was killed, the *Boston News Letter* published a detailed account of the pirate's last battle. Here it is:

Maynard and Teach themselves began the fight with their swords, Maynard making a thrust, the point of his sword went against Teach's cartridge box, and bended it to the hilt. Teach broke the guard of it, and wounded Maynard's fingers but did not disable him, whereupon he jumped back and threw away his sword and fired his pistol which wounded Teach. Demelt [another sailor] stuck in between them with his sword and cut Teach's face pretty much; in the interim [in the meantime] both companies engaged in Maynard's sloop, one of Maynard's men . . . engaged Teach with his broad sword, who gave Teach a cut on the neck, Teach saying well done lad; [the man] replied If it be not well done, I'll do it better. With that he gave him a second stroke, which cut off his head, laying it flat on his shoulder.

Shortly after Teach became the captain of his own ship, Thornigold gave up piracy. Captain Woodes Rogers, the British-appointed governor of the Bahamas, had been given the power to pardon pirates who agreed to mend their ways. Thornigold—and other members of Blackbeard's circle—sailed to New Providence to accept the King's pardon. Edward Teach, however, had just begun his short but active career as a pirate.

SMOKING BLACK BEARD

A tall man with a booming voice, Teach deliberately developed a terrifying appearance. He had an enormous black beard, which he tied up with black ribbons and twisted into braids. According to some accounts, it covered his entire face and grew down to his waist. Before going into battle, he tucked pieces of hempen rope (rope made from fibers of the hemp plant)—which were soaked in saltpeter and lit—into his hair. The slow-burning chords of rope gave off clouds of thick black smoke that gave him the appearance of a living demon. Captain Charles Johnson, the author of a pirate history that was published six years after Teach's death, wrote what is probably the best-known description of the infamous pirate:

Captain Teach assumed the cognomen [nickname] of Black-beard, from that large quantity of hair, which, like a frightful meteor, covered his whole face, and frightened America more than any comet that has appeared there in a long time.

This beard was black, which he suffered to grow of an extravagant length; as to breadth, it came up to his eyes; he was accustomed to twist it with ribbons, in small tails . . . and turn them about his ears: in time of action, he wore a sling over his shoulders,

Sunken history

In June of 1718, shortly before Teach was captured, his flagship—the *Queen Anne's Revenge*, a 103-foot forty-cannon vessel—became grounded on a sandbar off the coast of North Carolina. It eventually sank, taking with it secrets about the day-to-day existence of one of the world's most infamous sea robbers. But on November 21, 1996, one day before the anniversary of Teach's death in 1718, archaeologists found what they believe to be Teach's long lost flagship.

The wreck of the *Queen Anne's Revenge* probably doesn't contain any of the pirate's treasure. Historians believe that Teach had already hidden most of his loot, and anything else of value could easily have been stashed by the members of his crew as they jumped ship. What is most valuable about the find is the history that it may reveal—such as insights into the daily workings of life aboard a pirate ship. It may also fill in missing pieces about what is known of the eighteenth-century. For example, the chest full of medicines that the pirates received as a ransom payment could provide valuable clues about medicine and health care in Teach's day.

The wreck was discovered in just twenty feet of water two miles off the North Carolina coast near Beaufort, in an area called the "Graveyard of the Atlantic" because of the number of ships that are wrecked there. Towing an underwater metal detector over an eight-square-mile area, a team of archaeologists discovered numerous metal objects—including a bell dated 1709, large anchors, and a number of cannons. It may take four to five years to determine whether the wreck is what remains of the *Queen Anne's Revenge*, but evidence suggests that the submerged vessel is, in fact, the flagship of the infamous Edward Teach.

with three brace of pistols, hanging in holsters like bandoliers [a belt worn over the shoulder]; and stuck lighted matches under his hat, which appearing on each side of his face, his eyes naturally looking fierce and wild, made him altogether such a figure, that imagination cannot form an idea of a fury, from Hell, to look more frightful.

His actions also contributed to his reputation as a monster. He disemboweled (gutted) captives and fed their entrails to the sharks. He cut off the fingers of victims who were too slow to hand over their rings. He sliced up a prisoner's ears—and then forced him to eat them. What's more, he turned on his crew with no forewarning: he shot randomly at the pirates on his ship

A watery legend

After Teach was beheaded in his final battle on the *Jane,* his corpse was thrown into the sea. According to local legend, his headless body swam around the ship before disappearing into its murky grave.

Hidden treasure

According to legend, "Blackbeard's treasure" is buried at various spots along the eastern seaboard. But chances are, there is no such treasure: a typical pirate's plunder consisted of silk, cotton, tools, and assorted sailing supplies. Archaeologists are still hoping to recover the wreck of the *Adventure*—the vessel that carried the pirate to his last battle—and one other ship in his fleet. In those wrecks they hope to find not chests full of gold and jewels but a treasure of information on the age of piracy.

and marooned them when he didn't feel like sharing the bounty. Although there's no telling where the facts end and legend begins, it is probably safe to say that Blackbeard deserved his reputation as "the devil's brother."

THE CHARLESTON BLOCKADE

Like most pirates, there was a seasonal pattern to Teach's voyages. In the warmer months, his crew robbed ships off the coast of Virginia and the Carolinas. Operating out of Oracoke Inlet—off the island of Oracoke in the Outer Banks chain of islands that extends along the coast of North Carolina—his ships anchored in shallow waters that prevented other ships from attacking. As winter approached, Teach headed south, to the warmer climate of the Caribbean. Sailing on board his flagship, the *Queen Anne's Revenge,* he traveled with a fleet of other boats—many of which, like his, had been stolen and converted to pirate boats.

Having spent the winter of 1717 in the Caribbean, Teach's crew landed in Charleston, South Carolina, in the spring of 1718. With three other pirate sloops (small, one-masted ships), the pirates blockaded the city's harbor and attacked any ship that attempted to leave or enter. They also took prisoners and put ashore a landing party that had instructions to bring back medical supplies to treat diseases that plagued the crew. Teach promised to release the prisoners in exchange for the supplies. After he received a chest full of expensive medicine, he made good on his word (but not until after the captives had been robbed of their possessions). The governor of South Carolina described the incident in a report to officials in London, England:

> [The pirates] appeared in sight of the town, took our pilotboat and afterwards 8 or 9 sail with several of the best inhabitants of this place on board and then sent me word if I did not immediately send them a chest of medicines they would put every prisoner to death,

which for their sakes being complied with after plundering them of all they had were sent ashore almost naked. This company is commanded by one Teach alias Blackbeard has a ship of 40 odd guns under him and 3 sloops tenders besides and are in all above 400 men.

A ROYAL PAIN

Shortly after the Charleston blockade, the *Queen Anne's Revenge* sank. Sailing on another ship, a ten-gun vessel called the *Adventure,* Teach headed up the Pamlico River to the town of Bath in North Carolina—in search not of treasure but of a royal pardon. (England's King George I, who reigned from 1714 to 1727, offered to pardon pirates who gave up their profession. As a British colony, North Carolina was able to extend the king's pardon to pirates.) Charles Eden, the governor of North Carolina, granted Teach a pardon, and then ordered the court to declare him a privateer. As a privateer, Teach was able to continue to plunder ships in Carolina waters with no fear of being punished—provided he shared his loot with Governor Eden and his secretary and collector of customs, Tobias Knight. Sailing up and down the Pamlico River, Teach stole from ships he encountered as well as from local plantations.

Unable to appeal to Governor Eden for assistance, local traders asked Thomas Spotswood, the governor of Virginia, for protection from the pirates. In November 1718, Spotswood issued a proclamation offering rewards for the capture—dead or alive—of Teach and his shipmates. He also enlisted the help of British navy officers to organize an expedition to capture the infamous pirate, even though the Carolina shoreline was well beyond his jurisdiction.

BLACKBEARD'S LAST STAND

Under the charge of Lieutenant Robert Maynard, an experienced officer, two ships sailed to the Carolina coast with specific orders to rout the pirates (to search them out and force them

Privateers

During the War of the Spanish Succession between Spain, Britain, and France, many English seamen became privateers. Awarded a "letter of marque," they were given permission to attack Spanish merchant ships on England's behalf. It was, in effect, legalized piracy. But when the Treaty of Utrecht was signed in 1713—ending the War of Succession—many privateers and seamen lost their livelihood. And many, like Edward Teach, turned to piracy.

Walking the plank
Modern historians believe that pirates never really forced their victims to walk the plank--the punishment that has been associated with sea robbers for centuries.

to leave). Because the pirate ships were anchored in shallow waters that were difficult to navigate, Maynard took small vessels that had no guns, which meant his crew would be forced into hand-to-hand combat with knives and swords. Having learned from other seamen that Teach was anchored in a sheltered area off Oracoke Island, Maynard reached the area on the evening of November 21, 1718. Anchoring his ships nearby, he waited until morning to attack.

Maynard's ships—the *Jane* and the *Ranger*—headed for Oracoke Island at dawn. Spotting the approaching ships, the pirates sounded the alarm and pulled in the anchor. Maynard's vessels chased the pirate ships, using oars since there was very little wind to sail by. Navigating shallow waters that were filled with sand bars and submerged obstacles, Maynard's ships ran aground.

Next came a shouting match between the navy lieutenant and the pirate captain. In his pirate history, Captain Johnson describes the exchange:

> Black-Beard hail'd him in this rude Manner: Damn you for Villains, who are you? and from whence come you? The Lieutenant make him Answer, You may see by our Colours [the flags that identified a ship] we are no Pyrates. Black-beard bid him send his Boat on Board, that he might see who he was but Mr Maynard reply'd thus; I cannot spare my Boat, but

Opposite page: The fierce swordfight between Blackbeard, left, and Lieutenant Maynard.

Pirate skills

In order to succeed at sea roving, pirates needed to be familiar with the layout of coastlines—so that they could safely careen their ships (to run a ship ashore in order to clean the bottom of the vessel) or hide from pursuers. Most sailed close to shore, which required a detailed knowledge of the hazards that were hidden in shallow waters. Pirates also needed an understanding of predominating winds to ensure adequate sail-power.

I will come aboard of you as soon as I can, with my Sloop. Upon this Black- beard took a Glass of Liquor, & [and] drank to him with these Words: Damnation seize my Soul if I give you Quarters [a place to stay], or take any from you. In Answer to which, Mr Maynard told him, That he expected no Quarters from him, nor should he give him any.

Eventually, Maynard's crew managed to free its two vessels. Rowing toward Teach's ship, the crew was hit by a broadside volley that killed several men and wounded others. (Broadsides could be devastating: firing at the enemy, a ship discharged all the guns on one side of the boat at once—and at close range.) Maynard ordered the remainder of his crew to conceal itself below deck.

Teach assumed that most of Maynard's men had been killed by the broadside attack. But when he climbed aboard the *Jane,* he was surprised by Maynard's sailors. The fight that followed was Blackbeard's last battle. According to Captain Johnson's account, he "stood his ground and fought with great fury till he received five and twenty wounds." Of Teach's twenty-five wounds, the last was fatal: the pirate had been decapitated (beheaded). Maynard's crew threw Teach's headless corpse overboard—but the bearded head of the infamous pirate was hung from the bowsprit of Maynard's boat as a warning to other sea robbers. (A bowsprit is a large pole projecting from the front of a ship.) It also offered concrete proof of Teach's death—something that made it easier for Maynard to collect the reward on the pirate's head.

Sources for Further Reading

Broad, William. "Archaeologists Revise Portrait of Buccaneers as Monsters." *New York Times* (March 11, 1997), pp. C1, C9.

Cordingly, David. *Under the Black Flag.* New York: Random House, 1995, pp. 13–14, 20–21, 165–166, 191, 194–201.

"Cutthroat Dogs." *Current Events* (May 5, 1997), p. A2+.

"Devil of a Find." *People Magazine* (March 17, 1997), p. 114.

Nash, Jay Robert. *The Encyclopedia of World Crime.* Wilmette, IL: Crime Books, 1990, pp. 387–388.

Pirotta, Saviour. *Pirates and Treasures.* New York: Thomson Learning, 1995, pp. 27–31.

Platt, Richard. *Pirate.* New York: Alfred A. Knopf, 1994, pp. 30–31, 61.

"Sea May Have Yielded a Piece of Pirate Lore." *New York Times* (March 4, 1997), p. A14.

"Yo ho! Treasure!" *Time for Kids* (March 14, 1997), p. 65.

Anne Bonny

Born: c. 1700
Died: ?

Few women have been recorded in the histories of piracy. Because they were forbidden—by a pirate code—to sail on pirate vessels, they hid their identities. After Anne Bonny was captured in a battle with British naval officers, she became widely known—making her one of the few women whose life as a pirate has been documented.

A SAILOR'S WIFE

Born near Cork, Ireland, Bonny was the illegitimate (born out of wedlock) daughter of William Cormac, a successful lawyer. Her mother was the family's housemaid, Peg Brennan. When the scandal of having a baby out of wedlock affected the married attorney's legal practice, he sailed with Brennan and his daughter to America. Settling in Charleston in the British colony of South Carolina, he earned a fortune as a merchant and purchased a large plantation.

Peg Brennan died when Bonny was still a girl. As a teenager she married James Bonny, a poor sailor, against her father's will. Disowned, she was turned out of her father's house. In 1716 she sailed with her husband to the Caribbean island of New Providence, a safe shelter for pirates who preyed on the area's many merchant ships. The Bahama governor, Woodes Rogers, had been charged with ridding the area of pirates to ensure the safety of British ships. In an effort to reduce piracy, Rogers offered rewards to informants who provided information that led to the capture and conviction of pirates. James Bonny worked as a paid informant—an occupation of which his wife strongly disapproved.

WOMAN PIRATE

Governor Rogers soon changed his approach to the pirate problem: he offered a royal pardon to men who agreed to abandon piracy. Pirates flocked to New Providence to take advantage of the governor's amnesty (pardon). Among them was pirate captain John Rackam—known as "Calico Jack" for the colorful clothes he wore. Having arrived in New Providence in 1719, Rackam met Anne Bonny shortly after he accepted a royal pardon.

Bonny left her husband to live with Rackam—who offered to "buy" a divorce from James Bonny (a fairly common but very illegal practice at that time). James Bonny refused and informed the governor of his wife's infidelity. Rogers threatened to have Bonny flogged if she did not return to her husband, which prompted her to run away with Rackam. Together with some of Rackam's old crew, they overpowered the crew of a ship that was harbored at New Providence.

Bonny became a pirate—despite the pirate code that strictly forbade women to sail on pirate ships. Whether she hid the fact that she was a woman is disputed: the ship's quarters offered little privacy, and witnesses claimed that she sometimes wore dresses on board the pirate ship. According to reports, she was a strong and courageous woman who handled a cutlass (short curved sword) and pistol well. Rackam's crew included another woman pirate, Mary Read, who also wore men's clothing and was a brave fighter. The two women became good friends.

ENEMIES OF ENGLAND

Toward the end of summer in 1720, Rackam's crew attacked and boarded a British merchant ship called the *William.*

Pirate hunting

The governor of the Bahamas, Captain Woodes Rogers, was an experienced sea captain who had sailed around the world. Rogers was commissioned by the British government to break up the network of pirates who operated out of the Caribbean island of New Providence. He arrived in the West Indies in 1718 armed with three warships—and a proclamation from England's King George (1660–1727) that gave him the authority to pardon pirates.

Don't break the bargain

Many pirates took advantage of the pardon that Governor Rogers offered to men who swore to abandon their pirate ways. But the price of failure was high: those who continued to pirate ships were rounded up and hung.

Mary Read

Mary Read was born in England. Her father, a sailor, went to sea and never returned. No one knows what happened to him. Read's early life was in some ways similar to Anne Bonny's childhood. Like Bonny, she was probably an illegitimate child. Born after her father had disappeared, she was probably the daughter of a man who had an affair with her mother. Read's mother had another child—a boy—who died just before Read was born. After her son died, Read's mother dressed her daughter as a boy. By having Read pose as her legitimate son, she was able to collect an allowance from her mother-in-law.

Read's grandmother died when she was thirteen years old. With no allowance to help support her, she went to work. Still disguised as a boy, she was employed as a footman to a French woman. (A girl in a similar position would have been employed as a chambermaid.) Read didn't care for the life of a servant. According to Captain Johnson: "Here she did not live long, for growing bold and strong, and having also a roving mind, she entered herself on board a man-of-war [war ship], where she served some

Angered by Rackam's failure to fulfill his part of their pardon, Governor Rogers issued a proclamation that named Rackam—and the two women pirates—as enemies of England. The proclamation stated: "John Rackam and his said Company are hereby proclaimed Pirates and Enemies to the Crown of Great Britain, and are to be so treated and Deem'd by all his Majesty's subjects." The proclamation specifically named Bonny and Read as members of Rackam's "company."

For two months, Rackam's crew sailed on the stolen *William*. They attacked several fishing boats and merchant ships, and headed to the western side of Jamaica. Anchored in Negril Bay, the *William* encountered Captain Jonathon Barnet, who had been commissioned to round up pirates. Suspicious of Rackam's ship, Barnet approached the *William* at about ten o'clock in the evening. Unprepared for a fight, Rackam tried to flee. Barnet's well-armed boat overtook the pirates, and, firing at the ship, wrecked part of the *William*'s rigging (sailing gear), without which it was unable to escape. When Barnet's crew boarded the *William*, Bonny and Read were reportedly the only pirates who fought Barnet and his crew. Rackam and the entire pirate crew were captured and taken to jail.

time: then she quitted it, went over to Flanders and carried arms in a regiment of foot as a cadet." Involved in a number of skirmishes, Read earned praise from her superiors for her bravery.

Read fell in love with a Flemish soldier in her regiment. After their military campaign ended, she revealed her identity to the regiment and married the Flemish soldier. The couple moved to Breda, in the Netherlands, where they opened a pub (bar) called "The Three Horseshoes," whose main customers were officers from their old regiment. Business

flourished for a while. But Read's husband died suddenly and the soldiers left Breda shortly thereafter, taking with them most of the pub's business.

Posing again as a man, Read first joined a foot regiment of soldiers and then signed on board a Dutch ship headed for the Caribbean. The ship was taken over by pirates, and she eventually joined the crew led by John "Calico Jack" Rackam. But Read wasn't the only woman sea rover on Rackam's ship: Anne Bonny was a member of the pirate vessel's crew.

UNFINISHED SENTENCES

The pirates were tried in two separate trials. Rackam and ten of his crew men were tried in Spanish Town, Jamaica (known as St. Jago de la Vega), on November 16, 1720. Although they pleaded not guilty to the charges against them, they were all convicted and sentenced to be executed. Within the next two days, all eleven men were hanged. Before he was marched to the gallows, Rackam was reportedly allowed to see Bonny, who told him, "Had you fought like a man, you need not have been hanged like a dog!" After his execution, the body of Rackam was hung from a gibbet (a wooden frame) on Deadman's Cay—in plain view of passing ships.

Less than two weeks later, on November 28, Bonny and Read were tried for piracy. Dorothy Thomas, a witness at the trial, had been on a ship that was attacked by Rackam's crew. The two women pirates, she said, "wore men's jackets, and long trousers, and handkerchiefs tied about their heads," and "each of them had a machete [large heavy knife] and pistol in their hands." Thomas testified that the two women "cursed and swore at the men"—and urged them to kill her. There was no doubt that

Mary Read.

Bonny and Read had been willing participants in piracy. Convicted on two counts of piracy, they were sentenced to be hanged. Sir Nicholas Lawes sentenced them with these words:

You, Mary Read, and Anne Bonny, alias Bonn, are to go from hence to the place from whence you came, and from thence to the place of execution; where you shall be severally [each] hanged by the neck till you are severally dead. And God of his infinite mercy be merciful to both your souls.

Mercy is exactly what Bonny and Read requested from the court. Both claimed to be "quick with child" or pregnant. The judge postponed their execution until after they could be examined to determine whether they were telling the truth. Both women were found to be pregnant, and both escaped execution: under British law, a pregnant woman could not be executed. Read died in prison shortly after the trial, before her child was born. Bonny somehow disappeared from prison, leaving no record of what happened to her or her child.

Sources for Further Reading

Cordingly, David. *Under the Black Flag.* New York: Random House, 1995, pp. 57–65, 71, 177.

Langley, Andrew. *Twenty Names in Crime.* Tarrytown, NY: Marshall Cavendish, 1988, pp. 10–11.

Nash, Jay Robert. *The Encyclopedia of World Crime.* Wilmette, IL: Crime Books, 1990, pp. 432–434.

Nash, Jay Robert. *Look for the Woman, A Narrative Encyclopedia of Female Poisoners, Kidnappers, Thieves, Extortionists, Terrorists, Swindlers, and Spies, from Elizabethan Times to the Present.* New York: M. Evans, 1981, pp. 35–39.

Pirotta, Saviour. *Pirates and Treasures.* New York: Thomson Learning, 1995, pp. 30–31.

Other women pirates

Anne Bonny and Mary Read weren't the only women to become well-known pirates. The following women were notorious sea rovers in other areas of the world:

- Alvilda, the daughter of a Scandinavian king, organized an all-woman crew to avoid a forced marriage to the Danish prince Alf in the fifth century A.D. According to legend, Alvilda's ship ran into pirates who were so impressed by her that they made her their captain. Later, she was so taken by Prince Alf's ability in battle that she married him after all—and became the Queen of Denmark.

- The daughter of an Irish chieftain, Grace O'Malley was born around 1530. She led crews in a number of raids against other chieftains and she sometimes plundered merchant ships.

- Charlotte de Berry (born in England in 1636) dressed in men's clothes and served in the navy with her husband. After being forced on board a ship that was headed for Africa, she led a mutiny and took over the ship. She reportedly cut off the head of the ship's captain, who had assaulted her. De Berry led a number of attacks on gold-laden ships off the coast of Africa.

- Lady Kiligrew—the wife of Sir John Kiligrew, who was the vice-admiral of Cornwall, England—had pirates on both sides of the family. After engaging in a number of other attacks, she took over a German ship anchored in Falmouth harbor in the spring of 1582. Tried and convicted of piracy, she was sentenced to hang. Queen Elizabeth intervened, and Lady Kiligrew's sentence was reduced to a long imprisonment.

- In the early nineteenth century, a woman named Ching Shih led a large pirate fleet that plundered boats in the China Sea. She was in charge of about 1,800 ships—and 80,000 pirates.

Platt, Richard. *Pirate.* New York: Alfred A. Knopf, 1994, pp. 32–33.

Ross, Stewart. *Fact or Fiction, Pirates.* Surrey, British Columbia: Copper Beech, 1995, pp. 18–19.

Charles Gibbs

Born: c. 1800
Died: April 22, 1831

Although he lived almost one hundred years after the "golden age" of piracy, Charles Gibbs was a highly successful pirate who plundered tens of thousands of dollars in goods—and murdered with little hesitation.

A WANTED MAN

Born in Rhode Island at the end of the eighteenth century, Gibbs went to sea as a teenager. As a seaman during the War of 1812 (a conflict between the United States and Great Britain), he sailed with a number of privateers (legalized pirates), earning a reputation as an able fighter. Later, as a privateer aboard an Argentinean ship, Gibbs looted ships in the Caribbean.

By 1821 Gibbs had crossed the fine line that distinguished privateers from pirates. After signing on as a member of a ship's crew, he determined how he could best profit from his position. Taking advantage of a ship's brief stays in various ports, he stole goods and returned on board. If his ship carried valuable stock, he organized a mutiny (open rebellion against authority). With a help of a few other sailors, he typically murdered the captain and first mate—and any others who presented a threat to him.

Having become a notorious pirate, Gibbs was hunted by the U.S. Navy. The *Enterprise,* a military ship headed by Lieutenant Commander Lawrence Kearney, took over four of the pirate's ships—but Gibbs remained at large. With a hideout in Cuba, Gibbs captured ships throughout the Caribbean and reportedly led a comfortable life in New York City between sea rovings.

Gibbs eluded capture for more than ten years and earned a reputation as a fierce opponent as well as a dangerous ally (a person who joins forces with another). Rumors of his gruesome acts abounded: he was said to have set fire to an entire ship with the crew on board. And he was credited with having cut off the arms and legs of a captain who opposed him. After his capture, Gibbs bragged that by scaring off his co-pirates he was often able to keep all the stolen goods for himself. He also supposed that he had murdered some 400 victims, although historians believe his claim to be exaggerated.

PUBLIC HANGING

On November 1, 1830, Gibbs signed on board the *Vineyard* for a voyage from New Orleans, Louisiana, to Philadelphia, Pennsylvania. Just off Cape Hatteras, North Carolina, Gibbs organized a mutiny. Together with Thomas G. Wansley, the ship's cook, and three others, he took over the leadership of the *Vineyard* by murdering the captain, William Thornby, and first mate William Roberts. The pirates seized the ship's cargo. Valued at $50,000, it was Gibbs's biggest haul.

As the *Vineyard* sailed toward Philadelphia, the bodies of Thornby and Roberts were thrown overboard. Near Long Island, New York, the pirates scuttled (sank) the ship and headed inland. (Pirates scuttled ships by making holes in the bottom of the vessel. They often scuttled stolen ships they wanted to abandon.) The three sailors who had joined in the mutiny went to the authorities, claiming that they had joined Gibbs because they feared for their lives. Shortly thereafter, Gibbs and Wansley were captured and tried. In a sentence pronounced on March 11, 1831, the two were found guilty of murder and piracy.

Here's a book you might like:

Treasure Island, 1883, by Robert Louis Stevenson

Young Jim Hawkins is invited to serve as the cabin boy on a schooner headed for Treasure Island. Hawkins overhears some of the sailors—including the smooth-talking ship's cook, Long John Silver—as they plot a mutiny. But before he can warn the others, Treasure Island comes into view, and the ship's crew, armed with a map, scramble off to find the hidden treasure.

The hempen jig

Hanging was the traditional punishment for pirates. Wooden gallows were usually built for each hanging. Gallows were simple structures made of two upright beams that were joined at the top by a crossbeam. Hung from the crossbeam was the hangman's noose. Helped by the executioner, the prisoner stepped up a ladder that was leaned against the gallows. After the executioner placed the noose around the prisoner's neck, he awaited a signal—and then pushed the prisoner off the ladder.

The hanged man then fell until the rope became tight, which either broke his neck or slowly strangled him to death. Hanging was sometimes called "dancing the hempen jig" because hanged men sometimes "danced"—or convulsed—at the end of the hempen rope (rope made from fibers of the hemp plant) as they died. Sometimes a victim's friends or relatives pulled on his legs in order to hasten death. In some cases, such as the execution of the infamous Captain Kidd, the rope broke, and the half-dead pirate was forced to be hanged a second time.

In England and the colonies, pirates were hanged at the low-tide mark to indicate that their crimes had been committed under the jurisdiction of the Admiralty. Public hangings attracted large crowds, who gathered on the shore and in boats. A pirate's final words and confessions made interesting reading: they were usually printed and sold in the days following the execution.

Urged to confess before he died, Gibbs recounted a long series of horrible murders and other misdeeds, some of which he made up. Many of the terrible deeds he described, however, were true, and the pirate's final confession was printed in New York newspapers. On April 22, 1831, in front of thousands of people who watched from boats, Gibbs and Wansley were hanged on Ellis Island, New York. After the hanging, their corpses were given to the College of Physicians and Surgeons to be dissected (cut up for scientific examination).

Sources for Further Reading

Cordingly, David. *Under the Black Flag.* New York: Random House, 1995, pp. 145–146, 223–240.

Nash, Jay Robert. *The Encyclopedia of World Crime.* Wilmette, IL: Crime Books, 1990, p. 1307.

Pirotta, Saviour. *Pirates and Treasures.* New York: Thomson Learning, 1995, pp. 36–37.

Platt, Richard. *Pirate.* New York: Alfred A. Knopf, 1994, pp. 56–57.

Sifakis, Carl. *The Encyclopedia of American Crime.* New York: Facts on File, 1982, pp. 281–282.

Index

Italic type indicates volume number;
***boldface** indicates main entries and their page numbers;*
(ill.) indicates illustration.